P9-DBT-529

What king had 700 wives? *(See page 23)*

What prophet walked around naked for three years? *(See page 11)*

Who won the first beauty contest in the Bible? *(See page 15)*

Who was turned into a pillar of salt? *(See page 37)*

Who invented music-making? *(See page 75)*

What prophet was a very hairy man? *(See page 31)*

What people put gold chains around their camels' necks? *(See page 159)*

What prince had his hair cut just once a year? *(See page 31)*

Who used a stone for a pillow? *(See page 25)*

What demon-possessed man ran around naked? *(See page 11)*

. . . and more than 1,500 other challenging questions about the people in the Bible . . .

The Best of
Bible Trivia

⟨1⟩
KINGS
CRIMINALS
SAINTS &
SINNERS

J. STEPHEN LANG

LIVING BOOKS®
Tyndale House Publishers, Inc.
Wheaton, Illinois

Front cover illustrations by John Hayes
Photo of twins © 1989 by Robert Cushman Hayes
Photo of donkey by Animals Animals or Earth
Scenes © 1989 Margot Conte

*The Best of Bible Trivia I: Kings, Criminals,
Saints, and Sinners* is selections from *The
Complete Book of Bible Trivia,* copyright © 1988
by J. Stephen Lang, published by Tyndale House
Publishers, Inc.

Scripture quotations, unless otherwise noted, are
from the King James Version of the Bible.

Living Books is a registered trademark of Tyndale
House Publishers, Inc.

Library of Congress Catalog Card Number 89-51308
ISBN 0-8423-0464-9
Copyright © 1988 by J. Stephen Lang
All rights reserved
Printed in the United States of America

96 95 94 93 92 91 90
10 9 8 7 6 5 4 3

To Mark Fackler,
who is a friend of the Bible
and who understands laughter

Contents

Preface

Can we speak of *the Bible* and *trivia* in the same breath? Can this inspired document that is pored over with great seriousness by pastors, scholars, and lay people provide material for leisure—or even laughter?

I think it can, and as I began writing this book, I became more and more convinced that the Bible, the divine book through which God's Truth shines, is also an earthy, human collection of people and incidents that cannot help but amuse (as well as enlighten) a reader. I believe that the Bible has come down to us through God's initiative. I also believe that God chose to present his truth through stories, oracles, and letters that not only inspire us, but also captivate us as any good stories do. Even unbelievers have recognized for centuries that the Bible is a veritable treasure trove of stories, as attested to by the many poems, plays, novels, films, paintings, and sculptures that are based on the Scriptures.

The Bible throbs with human life. It is full of sublime teaching—and sometimes pathetic, sometimes amusing pictures of human failings. It evokes tears and laughter, repulsion and admiration. To probe its many characters and stories cannot be wrong. To ask questions about its content can, at the very least, provide innocent amusement. Even better, asking questions can lead us deeper into the content and make us appreciate and (it is hoped) study more deeply this fascinating treasury of stories.

This is not the first collection of questions and answers about the Bible, and it probably will not be the last.

However, most previous books seem to have focused on the seriousness of the text, neglecting the possibilities of finding things to chuckle over and cry over. Too many of these volumes have been painfully dry, with questions arranged in neat Genesis-to-Revelation sequence.

I have tried to avoid dryness at all costs. The arrangement here is topical, with such topics as "Laughers and Dancers," "Hairy and Hairless" (yes, really), "All Kinds of Villains," "Women on the Throne," and so on. I hope the choice of topics will itself provide some chuckles. And the category "Not to Be Taken Seriously" is just for laughs. One can't include *every* subject, of course, but the range is wide—priests, prostitutes, violent men, prisoners, warriors, prophets, liars, and many, many others. And while this volume of *The Best of Bible Trivia* focuses on the many interesting *people* in the Bible, Volumes II and III will cover many other subjects. In all, there are more than 1,500 questions arranged under more than 50 topical headings.

Though the questions are organized into categories, the book is meant for browsing. It was made to fill up your time commuting on the train, the hour you spend waiting at the dentist's office, the few minutes before dinner is on the table, the hours on the freeway when you and the other two people in the back seat are in the mood for a game of "quiz me." In other words, the book is designed to be read randomly, anywhere, and with no preparation of any kind. It is designed to entertain the person who unashamedly likes to be entertained—and challenged.

The author would like to hear from any person who is able to correctly (and without peeking at the answers on the back of each page) answer every question in this book. In doing the research for this book, the author himself learned quite a bit, but not enough to answer every question correctly—at least, not yet.

Happy reading! I hope you enjoy getting better acquainted with the divine—and very human—Book of books.

✦The Naked Truth

1. What prophet walked around naked for three years?
2. Who went naked as a way of wailing over the fate of Jerusalem?
3. What king of Israel, struck with the power to prophesy, stripped off his clothes and lay naked for a whole day and night?
4. What father lay naked and intoxicated in his tent, which so disturbed his sons that they came and covered him?
5. In war, what persons were often humiliated by being stripped?
6. What prophet threatened to take away the flax that covered his wife's nakedness?
7. What disciple, busy at his daily work, was caught naked by Jesus?
8. Who embarrassed his wife by shamelessly exposing himself while dancing for joy?
9. Where did a follower of Jesus escape an angry mob by running away naked?
10. What prophet spoke of a woman (merely a symbol) who committed sexual sins while naked?
11. What demon-possessed man ran around naked?

✦Laughers and Dancers

1. Whose dance proved fatal for John the Baptist?
2. Who held a feast with dancing when his son returned?

✦The Naked Truth (Answers)

 1. Isaiah (20:3).
 2. The prophet Micah (1:8).
 3. Saul (1 Samuel 19:24).
 4. Noah (Genesis 9:21-23).
 5. Captives (2 Chronicles 28:15).
 6. Hosea (2:3, 9).
 7. Simon Peter (John 21:7).
 8. King David (2 Samuel 6:20).
 9. Gethsemane (Mark 14:51-52).
10. Ezekiel (23:10, 29).
11. The Gerasene demoniac (Luke 8:27).

✦Laughers and Dancers (Answers)

 1. The daughter of Herodias (Matthew 14:6-8).
 2. The father of the prodigal son (Luke 15:25).

3. Who laughed at Nehemiah's plans to rebuild Jerusalem?

4. Who danced with all his might when the ark of the covenant was brought to Jerusalem?

5. Who laughed when she heard she would bear a son in her old age?

6. Who was snickered at for claiming that a dead girl was only asleep?

7. What prophetess led the women of Israel in a victory dance?

8. Whose ill-fated daughter came out dancing after his victory over the Ammonites?

9. Who had his decree for a Passover celebration laughed at by the men of Israel?

10. What tribe took wives from among the dancers at Shiloh?

11. Who came out dancing after David killed Goliath?

12. What old woman said, "God hath made me to laugh so that all who hear will laugh with me"?

13. Who told Job that God would certainly fill a righteous man with laughter?

14. What old man laughed at God's promise that he would father a child in his old age?

15. What group of people were busy dancing and partying when David caught up with them?

16. What graven image did the Israelites dance in front of?

17. Who, in the Beatitudes, does Jesus promise laughter to?

18. Whom did Jesus speak of as dancing in the streets?

19. Who danced around the altar of their false god?

20. Whose wife despised him for dancing in the streets?

21. According to Job, whose children dance about and make music?

22. What Old Testament character's name means "laughter"?

3. Sanballat, Tobiah, and Geshem (Nehemiah 2:19).
4. David (2 Samuel 6:14).
5. Sarah (Genesis 18:10-12).
6. Jesus (Matthew 9:23-24).
7. Miriam (Exodus 15:20).
8. Jephthah's (Judges 11:34).
9. Hezekiah (2 Chronicles 30:5, 10).
10. Benjamin (Judges 21:20, 23).
11. The women of Israel (1 Samuel 18:6-7).
12. Sarah (Genesis 21:6).
13. Bildad (Job 8:21).
14. Abraham (Genesis 17:17).
15. The Amalekites (1 Samuel 30:16-18).
16. The golden calf made by Aaron (Exodus 32:19).
17. Those who weep (Luke 6:21).
18. Children (Luke 7:32).
19. The priests of Baal (1 Kings 18:26).
20. David's wife, Michal (1 Chronicles 15:29).
21. The children of the wicked (Job 21:7-12).
22. Isaac (Genesis 21:3-6).

◆They Did It First

1. Who had the first birthday party in the Bible?
2. Where was the first beauty contest in the Bible, and who won?
3. Who was the first Christian martyr?
4. Who was the first drunk?
5. Who was the first person to fall asleep during a sermon?
6. Who used the first pseudonym?
7. Who built the first city?
8. Who was the first hunter?
9. Who was the first murderer?
10. What is the first book of the Bible named after a woman?
11. Who is the first prophet mentioned in the Bible?
12. Who was the first king of Israel?
13. Who were the first foreign missionaries?
14. Who was the first shepherdess?
15. Who was the first single man to be exiled?
16. Who was the first judge of Israel?
17. Who was the first disciple chosen by Jesus?
18. Who wore the first bridal veil?
19. Who was the first priest mentioned in Scripture?
20. Who wore the first ring?
21. Who took the first census of the Hebrews?
22. Who was the first shepherd?
23. Who were the first exiles?
24. Who were the first twins?
25. Who constructed the first altar?
26. Who built the first Jerusalem temple?
27. Who was the first metal craftsman?
28. Who was the first farmer?
29. Who was the first polygamist?
30. Who was the first apostle to be martyred?
31. Who was the first child mentioned in the Bible?
32. Who was the first daughter mentioned by name?
33. Who planted the first vineyard?

◆They Did It First (Answers)

1. Pharaoh, at the time Joseph was in Egypt (Genesis 40:20).
2. The one at the court of Persian ruler Ahasuerus. The winner was Esther (Esther 2).
3. Stephen (Acts 6:7—8:2).
4. Noah, who planted a vineyard after leaving the ark (Genesis 9:21).
5. Eutychus, who dozed off and fell out of a window during Paul's sermon (Acts 20:9).
6. Esther, whose real name was Hadassah (Esther 2:7).
7. Cain (Genesis 4:17).
8. Nimrod (Genesis 10:9).
9. Cain (Genesis 4:8).
10. Ruth.
11. Abraham (Genesis 20:7).
12. Saul (1 Samuel 10:1).
13. Paul and Barnabas (Acts 13).
14. Rachel (Genesis 29:9).
15. Cain (Genesis 4:12).
16. Othniel (Judges 3:9).
17. Simon Peter (John 1:42).
18. Rebekah (Genesis 24:65).
19. Melchizedek (Genesis 14:18).
20. Pharaoh (Genesis 41:42).
21. The priest Eleazar (Numbers 26:1-2).
22. Abel (Genesis 4:2).
23. Adam and Eve, driven from the garden (Genesis 3:24).
24. Jacob and Esau (Genesis 25:23-26).
25. Noah (Genesis 8:20).
26. Solomon (1 Kings 6).
27. Tubal-cain (Genesis 4:22).
28. Cain (Genesis 4:2).
29. Lamech (Genesis 4:19).
30. James (Acts 12:1-2).
31. Cain (Genesis 4:1).
32. Naamah, daughter of Lamech (Genesis 4:22).
33. Noah (Genesis 9:20).

✦Second in Line

1. At 969 years, Methuselah was the longest-lived man. Who came in second at 962 years?
2. Saul was the first king of Israel. Who was the second? (Hint: It wasn't David.)
3. The first covenant God made with man was his covenant with Noah. With whom did he make the second covenant?
4. In John's Gospel, Jesus' first miracle is turning water into wine. What is the second miracle?
5. Stephen was the first Christian martyr. What apostle was the second?
6. Paul's first traveling companion was Barnabas. Who was the second?
7. Othniel was the first judge of Israel. Who was the second?
8. Jacob's firstborn was Reuben. Who was his second son?
9. Eve is the first woman in the Bible. Who is the second?
10. Solomon led the way in constructing the first temple in Jerusalem. Who led in the building of the second temple?

✦Kings, Pharaohs, and Other Rulers

1. What king hosted a banquet where a phantom hand left a message on the palace wall?
2. What king of Israel was murdered while he was drunk?
3. What king of Salem was also a priest of the Most High God?
4. What king of Gerar took Sarah away from Abraham?

✦Second in Line (Answers)

1. Jared (Genesis 5:20).
2. Ishbosheth (2 Samuel 2:8-10).
3. Abraham (Genesis 15–17).
4. Healing an official's son in Cana (John 4:43-54).
5. James, brother of John (Acts 12:1-2).
6. Silas (Acts 15:36-41).
7. Ehud (Judges 3:15).
8. Simeon (Genesis 29:33).
9. Cain's wife, who is not named (Genesis 4:17).
10. Zerubbabel and Joshua (Ezra 3).

✦Kings, Pharaohs, and Other Rulers
(Answers)

1. Belshazzar (Daniel 5:1-9).
2. Elah (1 Kings 16:8-10).
3. Melchizedek (Genesis 14:18).
4. Abimelech (Genesis 20:2).

5. What Hebrew captive interpreted the dreams of the Egyptian pharaoh?
6. What three kings listened to the prophet Elisha as he prophesied to the accompaniment of a harp?
7. What king attacked the Israelites on their way into Canaan, only to be completely destroyed later?
8. What king of Sidon gave his daughter Jezebel as a wife to Ahab?
9. What king of Bashan was famous for having an enormous iron bed?
10. Who was the last king of Judah?
11. What king of Hazor organized an alliance against Joshua?
12. What military man captured 31 kings?
13. What king of Moab sent the prophet Balaam to curse Israel?
14. What king of Mesopotamia was sent by God to conquer the faithless Israelites?
15. What Canaanite king of the time of the judges was noted for having nine hundred iron chariots?
16. What son of Gideon was proclaimed king in Shechem?
17. What king of the Amalekites was captured by Saul and cut into pieces by Samuel?
18. What much-married king is considered the author of the Song of Songs?
19. What Philistine king did David seek refuge with when he fled from Saul?
20. What shepherd boy, the youngest of eight sons, was anointed by Samuel in front of his brothers?
21. What king wanted to see miracles when the arrested Jesus was sent to him?
22. What king of Tyre sent cedar logs and craftsmen to King David?
23. What prophet had a vision of a time when the Lord would gather the kings of the earth together and put them all in a pit?

5. Joseph (Genesis 41:1-36).
 6. Joram of Israel, Jehoshaphat of Judah, and the king of Edom (2 Kings 3:11-19).
 7. The king of Arad (Numbers 21:1-3).
 8. Ethbaal (1 Kings 16:31).
 9. Og (Deuteronomy 3:11).
10. Zedekiah (2 Kings 25:1-7).
11. Jabin (Joshua 11:1-5).
12. Joshua (12:9-24).
13. Balak (Numbers 22:2-6).
14. Cushan-Rishathaim (Judges 3:8).
15. Jabin (Judges 4:2-3).
16. Abimelech (Judges 9:6).
17. Agag (1 Samuel 15:8, 32).
18. Solomon (Song of Solomon 1:1).
19. Achish of Gath (1 Samuel 21:10).
20. David (1 Samuel 16:6-13).
21. Herod (Luke 23:8).
22. Hiram (2 Samuel 5:11).
23. Isaiah (24:21-22).

24. What man, David's oldest son, tried to make himself king of Israel?

25. What wise king made an alliance with Egypt when he married the pharaoh's daughter?

26. What Egyptian king gave refuge to Jeroboam when he fled from Solomon?

27. What king had a strange dream about an enormous, fruitful tree that is suddenly chopped down with only a dry stump left?

28. What man, one of Solomon's officials, had his reign over Israel foretold by the prophet Ahijah?

29. What king of Judah was constantly at war with King Jeroboam of Israel?

30. What king was confronted by the prophet Nathan because of his adulterous affair?

31. What king of Israel reigned only two years and was murdered while he was fighting against the Philistines?

32. What man violently protested having a king in Israel, though he himself anointed the first two kings?

33. What city did King Jeroboam use as his capital when the northern tribes split from the southern tribes?

34. What king of Israel reigned only seven days and killed himself by burning down his palace around him?

35. What king of Ethiopia was supposed to aid Hezekiah in breaking the power of the Assyrians?

36. What king led Israel into sin by allowing his evil wife to introduce Baal worship into the country?

37. Who was the last king of Israel?

38. What king of the Amorites refused to let the Israelites pass through his kingdom?

39. What king called Elijah the worst troublemaker in Israel?

40. What king of Syria was Elijah told to anoint?

41. What evil king of Judah was humbled and repentant after being taken to Babylon in chains?

24. Adonijah (1 Kings 1:5-53).
25. Solomon (1 Kings 3:1).
26. Shishak (1 Kings 11:40).
27. Nebuchadnezzar (Daniel 4:10-18).
28. Jeroboam (1 Kings 11:26-40).
29. Abijam, or Abijah (1 Kings 15:6).
30. David (2 Samuel 12:1-15).
31. Nadab (1 Kings 15:26-27).
32. Samuel (1 Samuel 8-10).
33. Tirzah (1 Kings 14:17).
34. Zimri (1 Kings 16:15, 18).
35. Tirhakah (2 Kings 19:9).
36. Ahab (1 Kings 16:29-33).
37. Hoshea (2 Kings 17:4).
38. Sihon (Numbers 21:21-26).
39. Ahab (1 Kings 18:17).
40. Hazael (1 Kings 19:15).
41. Manasseh (2 Chronicles 33:10-13).

42. What king was told by the prophet Micaiah that his troops would fall in battle?
43. What saintly king had a fleet built to sail for gold, though the ships never sailed?
44. What king of Israel consulted the god Baalzebub after falling off his palace balcony?
45. What king of Moab was famous as a sheep farmer?
46. What king refused to let the Israelites pass through his country on their way to Canaan?
47. What king had the prophet Uriah murdered for opposing him?
48. Who became king of Syria after he smothered King Ben-Hadad with a wet cloth?
49. What king of Judah led the country into sin by marrying the daughter of the wicked Ahab?
50. Who is the only king in the Bible referred to as "the Mede"?
51. What king had 700 wives?

✦So Many Dreamers

1. Who told Pilate that a worrisome dream made it clear that Pilate was to have nothing to do with Jesus?
2. According to one Old Testament prophet, there will come a day when young men will see visions and old men will dream dreams. Which prophet?
3. Who repeats the words of this prophet in an early Christian sermon?
4. Joseph, Mary's husband, was warned in dreams to do four things. What?
5. In Nebuchadnezzar's famous tree dream, who is symbolized by the majestic tree that is cut down?
6. Daniel had a dream of four beasts rising out of the sea. What did they look like?

42. Ahab (1 Kings 22:17).
43. Jehoshaphat (1 Kings 22:48).
44. Ahaziah (2 Kings 1:2).
45. Mesha (2 Kings 3:4).
46. The king of Edom (Numbers 20:14-20).
47. Jehoiakim (Jeremiah 26:20-23).
48. Hazael (2 Kings 8:15).
49. Jehoram (2 Kings 8:16-18).
50. Darius (Daniel 5:31).
51. Solomon (1 Kings 11:3).

✦So Many Dreamers (Answers)

1. His wife (Matthew 27:19).
2. Joel (2:28).
3. Peter, at Pentecost (Acts 2:17).
4. Go ahead and marry Mary, take a different route out of Bethlehem, flee to Egypt, return from Egypt (Matthew 1:18–2).
5. Nebuchadnezzar (Daniel 4:5-17).
6. A lion, a bear, a leopard, and a monster with iron teeth (Daniel 7).

7. In Nebuchadnezzar's dream of the statue, what four metals are mentioned as composing the statue?

8. One of Gideon's soldiers dreamed of a Midianite tent being overturned by an unlikely object. What was it?

9. When God came to the young Solomon in a dream and asked him what he desired, what did Solomon ask for?

10. What three Egyptian officials did Joseph interpret dreams for?

11. God protected Jacob by sending a dream of warning that Jacob should not be pursued or harmed. Who received this dream?

12. Who irritated his brothers by telling them of his dreams?

13. Who slept on a stone pillow at Bethel and had a dream of a stairway to heaven?

◆Change of Life, Change of Name

What were the original names of these biblical characters?

1. Abraham and Sarah
2. Israel
3. Joshua
4. Solomon
5. Peter
6. Paul
7. Mara
8. Zaphnath-paaneah
9. Belteshazzar
10. Jehoiakim
11. Zedekiah

7. Gold, silver, brass, and iron (Daniel 2:31-35).
8. A cake of barley bread (Judges 7:13).
9. An understanding heart and good judgment (1 Kings 3:5-10).
10. The pharaoh, his baker, and his butler (Genesis 40—41).
11. Laban, Jacob's father-in-law (Genesis 31:29).
12. Joseph (Genesis 37:2-11).
13. Jacob (Genesis 28:10-15).

◆Change of Life, Change of Name (Answers)

1. Abram and Sarai (Genesis 17:5, 15).
2. Jacob (Genesis 32:28).
3. Oshea (Numbers 13:16).
4. Jedidiah (2 Samuel 12:24-25).
5. Simon, or Simeon (John 1:42).
6. Saul (Acts 13:9).
7. Naomi (Ruth 1:20).
8. Joseph (Genesis 41:45).
9. Daniel (1:6-7).
10. Eliakim (2 Kings 23:34).
11. Mattaniah (2 Kings 24:17).

✦What's in a Name?

Most biblical names had specific meanings. Below are the meanings of the names of several biblical characters. Can you name the person in each case? (This isn't as hard as it looks. Except for 1, 2, 4, 6, and 9-14, all the names are found in the titles of books of the Bibles. The other names are also familiar.)

1. beloved
2. prosperous
3. God is strong
4. God is savior
5. help
6. great warrior
7. love's embrace
8. salvation of the Lord
9. God has helped
10. red earth
11. eagle
12. enlightened
13. the Lord sustains
14. the Lord is gracious
15. messenger
16. worshiper of the Lord
17. the Lord has consoled
18. star
19. something worth seeing
20. asked of God
21. exalted of God
22. dove
23. he that weeps
24. peace
25. honored of God
26. honorable
27. God is judge
28. the Lord is salvation

◆What's in a Name? (Answers)

1. David
2. Festus
3. Ezekiel
4. Elisha
5. Ezra
6. Gideon
7. Habakkuk
8. Isaiah
9. Lazarus
10. Adam
11. Aquila
12. Aaron
13. Ahaz
14. Ananias
15. Malachi
16. Obadiah
17. Nehemiah
18. Esther
19. Ruth
20. Samuel
21. Jeremiah
22. Jonah
23. Job
24. Solomon
25. Timothy
26. Titus
27. Daniel
28. Joshua

29. salvation
30. one with a burden
31. gift of the Lord
32. light-giving
33. rock
34. the Lord remembers
35. little
36. the Lord hides
37. the Lord has been gracious
38. praise of the Lord
39. festive
40. who is like the Lord
41. compassionate
42. affectionate
43. the Lord is God
44. polite
45. supplanter

◆Names Made in Heaven

1. What did God change Jacob's name to?
2. Who was told by God to name his son Maher-shalal-hash-baz?
3. Who told Joseph what Jesus' name would be?
4. What prophet was told by God to name his son Lo-ammi?
5. Who told Hagar to name her son Ishmael?
6. What did God change Abram's name to?
7. Who was told by an angel that his son was to be named John?
8. What prophet told the priest Pashur that his new name was to be Magor-missabib?
9. What did God call his human creation?
10. What new name did Jesus give to Simon?
11. What was Hosea told to name his daughter?
12. What was Sarai's name changed to?

29. Hosea
30. Amos
31. Matthew
32. Luke
33. Peter
34. Zechariah
35. Paul
36. Zephaniah
37. John
38. Jude
39. Haggai
40. Micah
41. Nahum
42. Philemon
43. Joel
44. Mark
45. James

✦Names Made in Heaven (Answers)

1. Israel (Genesis 32:28).
2. Isaiah (8:3).
3. An angel (Matthew 1:20-21).
4. Hosea (1:9).
5. An angel (Genesis 16:11).
6. Abraham (Genesis 17:5).
7. Zacharias (Luke 1:13).
8. Jeremiah (20:3).
9. Adam (Genesis 5:2).
10. Peter (John 1:42).
11. Lo-ruhamah (Hosea 1:6).
12. Sarah (Genesis 17:15).

13. Who was told to name his son Solomon?
14. Who was told to name his firstborn son Jezreel?
15. Who told Mary that her son was to be named Jesus?

✦Hairy and Hairless

1. What prophet was a very hairy man?
2. Who is the only man mentioned in the Bible as being naturally bald?
3. What grief-stricken Old Testament man shaved his head after he learned his children had been destroyed?
4. What king of Babylon, driven from his palace, lived in the wilderness and let his hair grow long and shaggy?
5. Who is mentioned first in the Bible as being very hairy?
6. What son of David had his hair cut once a year, the amount of the hair weighing two hundred shekels?
7. What apostle purified himself, along with four other men, by shaving his head?
8. As a Nazarite, this judge of Israel never shaved or had a haircut until his mistress shaved his head. Who was he?
9. What leader plucked out his own hair and beard when he heard the Jews had intermarried with other races?
10. What smooth-skinned man had a hairy twin brother?
11. What sort of person had to shave all his hair twice, six days apart?
12. Who was forbidden to "round the corners of the head"?
13. What class of people could not shave their heads nor let their hair grow long?
14. What prophet did God tell to shave his head and beard?

13. David (1 Chronicles 22:9).
14. Hosea (1:4).
15. The angel Gabriel (Luke 1:30-31).

✦**Hairy and Hairless** (Answers)

1. Elijah (2 Kings 1:8).
2. Elisha (2 Kings 2:23).
3. Job (1:20).
4. Nebuchadnezzar (Daniel 4:33).
5. Esau (Genesis 27:11-23).
6. Absalom (2 Samuel 14:26).
7. Paul (Acts 21:23-26).
8. Samson (Judges 16:17).
9. Ezra (9:1-3).
10. Jacob, brother of Esau (Genesis 27:11-22).
11. A leper (Leviticus 14:7-9).
12. Jews (Leviticus 19:27).
13. Priests (Ezekiel 44:20).
14. Ezekiel (5:1-4).

15. Who was so incensed at the intermarriage of Jews with foreigners that he pulled out the hair of some men?
16. What prophet told the people of Jerusalem to cut off their hair as a sign the Lord had rejected them?
17. Who had to shave their whole bodies as part of the ceremony of consecrating themselves to the Lord?
18. If an Israelite man took a woman prisoner of war as his wife, what did she have to do to her hair?
19. What group of consecrated men never cut their hair?
20. What Christian shaved his head at Cenchrea in connection with a vow?

◆The Runners

1. What bizarre person saw Jesus from far off and ran to worship him?
2. What belligerent man ran to meet his brother and kissed him after a long time of separation?
3. What prophet outran a king's chariot and a team of horses?
4. What evangelist ran to meet a foreign official in his chariot?
5. What disciple outran Peter to Jesus' tomb?
6. Who ran to the priest Eli, thinking Eli had called him in the night, though it was actually God who called?
7. What cousin of Jacob's ran to tell her father when she found she and Jacob were related?
8. What boy ran into the Philistine camp to confront their best warrior?
9. What servant of the prophet Elisha ran to meet the woman of Shunem?
10. What short man ran to see Jesus but could not because of his height?
11. Who ran to meet the Lord in the plains of Mamre?

15. Nehemiah (13:23-27).
16. Jeremiah (7:29).
17. The Levites (Numbers 8:5-7).
18. Shave it off (Deuteronomy 21:10-12).
19. The Nazarites (Numbers 6:5, 13, 18).
20. Paul (Acts 18:18).

◆The Runners (Answers)

1. The Gadarene demoniac (Mark 5:6).
2. Esau (Genesis 33:4).
3. Elijah (1 Kings 18:46).
4. Philip (Acts 8:30).
5. John (John 20:4).
6. Samuel (1 Samuel 3:4-5).
7. Rachel (Genesis 29:12).
8. David (1 Samuel 17:48-49).
9. Gehazi (2 Kings 4:25-26).
10. Zacchaeus (Luke 19:4).
11. Abraham (Genesis 18:1-2).

12. Who sent Cushi to run to David with the news of Absalom's death?

13. According to Isaiah, what sort of person can run and not be weary?

14. What prophet ran after another prophet to accept the appointment as his successor?

15. What usurper to the throne of Israel gathered up fifty men to run before him?

16. When the man of Benjamin saw the ark of the covenant captured by the Philistines, what Israelite did he run to tell?

17. What judge's mother ran to tell her husband Manoah that an angel had appeared to her?

18. What beautiful woman caused Abraham's servant to run to meet her?

19. What did a man at Jesus' crucifixion run to find for the dying Jesus?

20. Who ran into the midst of the Israelites carrying incense to stop a plague?

21. Who had a vision of one angel running to meet another?

22. What two women ran from Jesus' empty tomb to tell the disciples what had happened?

23. What man ran to meet Abraham's servant at the well?

✦Notable Women, and Some Less Notable (I)

1. The only female judge of Israel, she judged the tribes from under a palm tree. Her victory song is famous. Who was she?

2. What widowed prophetess was eighty-four years old when she saw the young Jesus in the temple?

12. Joab (2 Samuel 18:19-23).
13. They that wait upon the Lord (Isaiah 40:31).
14. Elisha (1 Kings 19:19-21).
15. Adonijah (1 Kings 1:5).
16. The priest Eli (1 Samuel 4:12-18).
17. Samson's (Judges 13:10).
18. Rebekah (Genesis 24:17).
19. A sponge (Matthew 27:46-48).
20. Aaron (Numbers 16:46-48).
21. Zechariah (2:3).
22. Mary and Mary Magdalene (Matthew 28:8).
23. Laban (Genesis 24:29).

✦Notable Women, and Some Less Notable (I) (Answers)

1. Deborah (Judges 4-5).
2. Anna (Luke 2:36-38).

3. What wife of David had been married to Nabal, who died when she told him of the gifts she had given to David?

4. What elderly cousin of Mary became the mother of John the Baptist?

5. What prophetess, active during the reign of Josiah, consoled the king while chastising the people of Judah?

6. What scheming princess of Tyre married and manipulated the weak Ahab and imposed her pagan religion on Israel?

7. What Israelite woman aided the people by murdering the Canaanite captain Sisera in her tent?

8. What Jewish girl married a Persian emperor and helped save her exiled people from extermination?

9. What two sisters of Bethany had a brother named Lazarus and were close friends of Jesus?

10. What prophetess was the sister of two great leaders and was once afflicted with leprosy for being rebellious?

11. What harlot became a hero for saving the life of Joshua's spies and was so honored in later days that she is listed in the genealogy of Jesus?

12. What loving woman, a concubine of Saul, watched over the corpses of her slaughtered children, protecting them from birds and animals?

13. Though her profession was condemned by an official decree of King Saul, the king disguised himself in order to get help from her. Who was she?

14. What Persian queen upset the king and his counselor by refusing to appear before them at their drunken banquet?

15. What dancer so enchanted Herod that he offered her anything she wished?

16. Who was turned into a pillar of salt?

17. What king of Judah was Abi the wife of?

18. What sister of David had the same name as one of David's wives?

3. Abigail (1 Samuel 25:18-20).
 4. Elisabeth (Luke 1).
 5. Huldah (2 Kings 22:14-20).
 6. Jezebel (1 Kings 16—19).
 7. Jael (Judges 4:17-22).
 8. Esther.
 9. Mary and Martha (Luke 10:38-42; John 11).
10. Miriam (Exodus 15; Numbers 12).
11. Rahab (Joshua 2, 6).
12. Rizpah (2 Samuel 21:1-10).
13. The witch of Endor (1 Samuel 28).
14. Vashti (Esther 1).
15. The daughter of Herodias, known to us from the writings of Josephus as Salome, though her name does not appear in the Bible (Matthew 14:1-11).
16. Lot's wife (Genesis 19:26).
17. Ahaz (2 Kings 18:2).
18. Abigail (1 Chronicles 2:16-17).

19. What woman was given as a wife after her future husband brought in two hundred Philistine foreskins as a gift to her father?

20. Who offered a bottle of milk to an enemy soldier and then killed him?

21. After Eve, who is the first woman mentioned in the Bible?

22. What Old Testament woman had children named Lo-ruhamah, Lo-ammi, and Jezreel?

23. What was Saul's wife's name?

24. What wife of David was also given as a wife to a man named Phaltiel?

25. What woman of Corinth had a household that Paul described as being full of strife among Christian leaders?

26. What woman was, in Ezekiel, used as a symbol of wicked Jerusalem?

27. What woman with a cumbersome name was the Hittite wife of Esau?

28. Who is the only woman mentioned in Paul's letter to Philemon?

29. What Egyptian woman was the wife of Joseph?

30. Who was the mother of the Levitical priesthood?

31. What king of Judah was the husband of Azubah?

32. What Hittite woman married Esau, causing grief to Isaac and Rebekah?

33. What handmaid of Rachel bore Jacob the sons Dan and Naphtali?

34. What daughter of a pharaoh married one of the descendants of Judah?

35. What woman was, in Ezekiel, used as a symbol of wicked Samaria?

36. What woman of Rome was mentioned by Paul as sending her greetings to Timothy?

37. What wife of David was the mother of the rebellious Adonijah?

38. What woman of Midian was killed by being run through with a javelin?

19. Michal (1 Samuel 18:27).
20. Jael (Judges 4).
21. Adah (Genesis 4:19).
22. Gomer, wife of Hosea (Hosea 1).
23. Ahinoam (1 Samuel 14:50).
24. Michal (1 Samuel 25:44).
25. Chloe (1 Corinthians 1:11).
26. Aholibah (Ezekiel 23:4, 11).
27. Aholibamah (Genesis 36:2, 5).
28. Apphia, a Christian of Colossae (Philemon 2).
29. Asenath (Genesis 41:45).
30. Elisheba, wife of Aaron (Exodus 6:23).
31. Asa (1 Kings 22:41-42).
32. Bashemath (Genesis 26:34).
33. Bilhah (Genesis 29:29; 30:3-7; 35:22, 25; 37:2).
34. Bithiah (1 Chronicles 4:18).
35. Aholah (Ezekiel 23:4-5).
36. Claudia (2 Timothy 4:21).
37. Haggith (2 Samuel 3:4).
38. Cozbi (Numbers 25:15-18).

39. What woman of Athens became a Christian because of Paul's teaching?

40. What Egyptian woman was the mother of two of the tribes of Israel?

41. What two women of Philippi are asked by Paul to stop their quarreling?

42. Who were the first two women to be the wives of the same man?

43. What was Esther's Hebrew name?

44. What was the name of Sarah's Egyptian maid?

45. What did Naomi call herself after suffering great tragedy?

46. What Egyptian servant woman was insolent to Sarah?

47. What Midianite woman was slain by the priest Phinehas for marrying an Israelite?

48. Who was wife to godly King Josiah?

49. What queen of Judah was the wife of godly King Hezekiah and mother of evil King Manasseh?

50. What wife of Lamech was the mother of the founder of music?

51. What courageous woman was wife of the priest Jehoiada?

52. Who had a daughter named Jemima?

53. What daughter of a priest married a king who became a leper?

54. What evil woman is associated with the church of Thyatira?

55. What woman, the wife of a servant of Herod, was healed by Jesus?

56. What woman of the Roman church is commended by Paul for her hard work?

57. Who had a wife named Judith?

58. What church was Julia part of?

59. Who had a daughter named Keren-happuch?

60. Who was Abraham's wife after Sarah died?

61. What two Hebrew women did God make houses for?

62. What prophet had a daughter named Lo-ruhamah?

39. Damaris (Acts 17:34).
40. Asenath, mother of Manasseh and Ephraim (Genesis 46:20).
41. Eudodia and Syntyche (Philippians 4:2).
42. Adah and Zillah, wives of Lamech (Genesis 4:19-24).
43. Hadassah (Esther 2:7).
44. Hagar (Genesis 16:1).
45. Mara (Ruth 1:20).
46. Hagar (Genesis 16:3-5).
47. Cozbi (Numbers 25:15-18).
48. Hamutal (2 Kings 23:31).
49. Hephzibah (2 Kings 21:1).
50. Adah (Genesis 4:19-23).
51. Jehosheba (2 Kings 11:2).
52. Job (42:14).
53. Jerusha, wife of Uzziah (2 Kings 15:32-33).
54. Jezebel (Revelation 2:20).
55. Joanna (Luke 8:2-3).
56. Mary (Romans 16:6).
57. Esau (Genesis 26:34).
58. The church at Rome (Romans 16:15).
59. Job (42:14).
60. Keturah (Genesis 25:1).
61. Puah and Shiprah, the midwives (Exodus 1:20-21).
62. Hosea (1:6, 8).

63. What wife of David was mother of the handsome—but rebellious—Absalom?

64. What daughter of Absalom married her cousin, King Rehoboam?

65. What servant woman was ordered out of the house by Sarah?

66. What wife of a palace official went to embalm the body of Jesus?

67. Who was Mehetabel?

68. What daughter of Saul was promised as a wife to David for slaying Goliath?

69. Who was the mother of Huz, Buz, and Pildash?

70. Who is the first daughter mentioned by name in the Bible?

71. What Ammonite woman, a wife of Solomon, became the mother of royal dynasty of Judah?

72. What Israelite woman lived in Moab but returned to Israel after her husband's death?

73. What false prophetess made attempts to keep Nehemiah from rebuilding the walls of Jerusalem?

74. Who was Ruth's sister-in-law?

75. What church was the faithful Persis a part of?

76. Who were Puah and Shiprah?

77. What four women in the early church were described as prophetesses?

78. What servant girl in Jerusalem came to the door when Peter escaped from prison?

79. What Hebrew woman married an Egyptian and later saw their half-breed son stoned to death?

80. What man's daughters involved him in incestuous relations when they believed there were no other men around?

63. Maacah (2 Samuel 3:3).
64. Maachah (1 Kings 15:2).
65. Hagar (Genesis 21:10-14).
66. Joanna (Luke 24:10).
67. Wife of Hadad, a king of Edom (Genesis 36:39).
68. Merab (1 Samuel 18:17-19).
69. Milcah (Genesis 22:20-22).
70. Naamah, daughter of Lamech (Genesis 4:22).
71. Naamah (1 Kings 14:21).
72. Naomi (Ruth 1).
73. Noadiah (Nehemiah 6:14).
74. Orpah (Ruth 1:4).
75. Rome (Romans 16:12).
76. Hebrew midwives at the time of Moses' birth (Exodus 1:15).
77. The daughters of Philip (Acts 21:8-9).
78. Rhoda (Acts 12:13).
79. Shelomith (Leviticus 24:10-23).
80. Lot's (Genesis 19:30-38).

✦More Kings, Pharaohs, and Other Rulers

1. What king of Israel had a reputation as a fast and furious chariot driver?
2. What king did Esther marry?
3. What Syrian king besieged Samaria, causing great famine that led to cannibalism?
4. What Egyptian king fought against Judah and murdered King Josiah?
5. What king of Judah had to be hidden as a boy to protect him from the wrath of wicked Queen Athaliah?
6. Who set up golden bulls at Dan and Bethel so that his people would not go to Jerusalem to worship?
7. What good king of Judah was murdered by two of his court officials?
8. What king of Israel made Elisha angry by not striking the ground enough with his arrows?
9. What king of Judah showed mercy when he executed his father's murderers but spared their families?
10. What king ran a beauty contest to pick a bride and wound up marrying a Jewish girl?
11. What king of Judah was stricken with leprosy?
12. What king of Israel was assassinated by Shallum after a six-month reign?
13. What cruel king of Israel assassinated King Shallum and ripped open the pregnant women of Tappuah?
14. What king of Egypt received an appeal for help from Hoshea of Israel, who wanted to throw off the Assyrian yoke?
15. What king of Israel had much of his territory taken away by the Assyrian king?
16. What evil king of Judah sacrificed his son as a burnt offering and built a Syrian-style altar in Jerusalem?
17. What king of Israel experienced a long famine and drought during his reign?

✦More Kings, Pharaohs, and Other Rulers

(Answers)

1. Jehu (2 Kings 9:20).
2. Ahasuerus, also known as Xerxes (Esther 1:1).
3. Ben-Hadad (2 Kings 6:24-30).
4. Neco (2 Kings 23:29).
5. Joash (2 Kings 11:2).
6. Jeroboam (1 Kings 12:26-31).
7. Joash (2 Kings 12:20-21).
8. Jehoash (2 Kings 13:18-19).
9. Amaziah (2 Kings 14:5-6).
10. Ahasuerus, or Xerxes (Esther 2:1-18).
11. Uzziah, also called Azariah (2 Kings 15:5).
12. Zechariah (2 Kings 15:8-10).
13. Menahem (2 Kings 15:16).
14. So (2 Kings 17:4).
15. Pekah (2 Kings 15:29).
16. Ahaz (2 Kings 16:3, 10).
17. Ahab (1 Kings 18:1-2).

18. What Assyrian king brought about the fall of Samaria and the deportation of the Israelites to other countries?

19. What godly king of Judah tore down the idols in the country and broke the power of the Philistines?

20. What king of Gezer opposed Joshua's army and was totally defeated, with no soldiers left alive?

21. What Assyrian king was killed by his sons while worshiping in the temple of his god Nisroch?

22. What king was criticized by the prophet Isaiah for showing Judah's treasure to Babylonian ambassadors?

23. What king of Syria joined the king of Israel in attacking Judah?

24. What Assyrian king received thirty-eight tons of silver as tribute money from Menahem of Israel?

25. What king of Assyria had his army of 185,000 soldiers destroyed by the angel of the Lord?

26. What cruel king lied to the wise men about his desire to worship the infant Jesus?

27. What king of Judah had the worst reputation for killing innocent people?

28. What king of Judah reigned for only two years and was murdered by his court officials?

29. What godly king began his reign at age eight and led a major reform movement in Judah?

30. Who had a dream about a statue composed of different materials?

31. What king reinstituted the celebration of Passover in Judah and invited the people of Israel to participate?

32. What king of Judah was killed at the Battle of Megiddo by the forces of Egypt?

33. What king repented because of the preaching of the prophet Jonah?

34. What king of Israel tricked the worshipers of Baal by gathering them together in a temple and slaughtering all of them?

18. Shalmaneser (2 Kings 17:3-6).
19. Hezekiah (2 Kings 18:1-8).
20. Horam (Joshua 10:33).
21. Sennacherib (2 Kings 19:36-37).
22. Hezekiah (2 Kings 20:12-18).
23. Rezin (2 Kings 16:5).
24. Tiglath-Pileser (2 Kings 16:7-8).
25. Sennacherib (2 Kings 19:35).
26. Herod (Matthew 2:7-8).
27. Manasseh (2 Kings 21:16).
28. Amon (2 Kings 21:19-23).
29. Josiah (2 Kings 22–23).
30. Nebuchadnezzar (Daniel 2).
31. Hezekiah (2 Chronicles 30:1-12).
32. Josiah (2 Kings 23:29-30).
33. The king of Nineveh (Jonah 3:6).
34. Jehu (2 Kings 10:18-27).

35. What king of Israel built the city of Samaria and made it his capital?

36. What Babylonian king sent his ambassadors to the court of Hezekiah, where they were shown all his treasures?

37. What son of Josiah was taken prison by Pharaoh Neco and never left Egypt?

38. Who reigned in Jerusalem when the Babylonian king's forces first attacked Judah?

39. Who was reigning in Judah when the Babylonians besieged Jerusalem and carried the nobles of the city away to Babylon?

40. What king of Judah saw the country threatened by the Assyrian army of Sennacherib?

41. What king of Babylon burned down the temple, palace, and city walls of Jerusalem?

42. What king of Judah was blinded and taken away in chains to Babylon?

43. Who was taken prisoner to Babylon, though he came to enjoy the favor of the Babylonian king?

44. What Babylonian king gave the deposed king of Judah a place of great honor in Babylon?

45. What king burned in his fireplace the letter sent to him by the prophet Jeremiah?

46. What king ordered Jezebel's servants to toss her out of a window?

47. What king of Persia issued the decree that the people of Judah could rebuild their temple?

48. What king of Assyria had sent foreigners to settle in Israel after the Israelites had been taken away?

49. What Persian king received a letter complaining about the Jews rebuilding their temple in Jerusalem?

50. What soldier was anointed king of Israel by one of Elisha's followers?

35. Omri (1 Kings 16:24).
36. Merodach-Baladan (2 Kings 20:12-13).
37. Joahaz, or Jehoahaz (2 Kings 23:33-34).
38. Jehoiakim (2 Kings 24:1).
39. Jehoiachin (2 Kings 24:15-16).
40. Hezekiah (2 Kings 18:13).
41. Nebuchadnezzar (2 Kings 25:8-11).
42. Zedekiah (2 Kings 25:7).
43. Jehoiachin (2 Kings 25:27-30).
44. Evilmerodach (2 Kings 25:27-30).
45. Jehoiakim (Jeremiah 36:23).
46. Jehu (2 Kings 9:31-33).
47. Cyrus (Ezra 1:1-4).
48. Esarhaddon (Ezra 4:2).
49. Artaxerxes (Ezra (4:6-7).
50. Jehu (2 Kings 9:1-10).

✦Women on the Throne

1. Who plotted the execution of John the Baptist?
2. Bernice was the consort of what ruler?
3. The Ethiopian eunuch that Philip witnessed to was the servant of what queen?
4. Whose wife brought Daniel's gift of prophecy to her husband's attention?
5. What Jewish girl became queen of Persia?
6. Who defied her royal husband and was replaced by a foreign woman?
7. What daughter of Ahab tried to destroy the entire royal line of Judah?
8. Who was removed from her position as queen mother because she had made an idol?
9. What Baal-worshiping princess led Ahab into idolatry?
10. During the reigns of David and Solomon, Tahpenes was the queen of what country?
11. What queen traveled far to meet Solomon face to face?
12. What wife of the soldier Uriah became David's wife and bore him Solomon?
13. Rizpah was the wife of what king of Israel?
14. Who became David's wife after her husband, Nabal, died?
15. Who nagged at David for dancing in the streets?

✦Most Mentioned Men

1. What man, as if you didn't know, is the most mentioned man in the Bible?
2. What king, mentioned 1118 times in the Bible, is the second most mentioned man?
3. What leader, with 740 mentions, ranks third?

✦Women on the Throne (Answers)

1. Herodias, wife of Herod (Matthew 14:3-8).
2. King Agrippa (Acts 25:13).
3. Candace (Acts 8:27-38).
4. Belshazzar's (Daniel 5:10).
5. Esther (Esther 2:17).
6. Vashti (Esther 1:11).
7. Athaliah (2 Chronicles 22:10).
8. Maacah (2 Chronicles 15:16).
9. Jezebel (1 Kings 16:31).
10. Egypt (1 Kings 11:19).
11. The queen of Sheba (1 Kings 10:1).
12. Bathsheba (2 Samuel 11-12).
13. Saul (2 Samuel 3:7).
14. Abigail (1 Samuel 25:39).
15. Michal (1 Samuel 18:20; 2 Samuel 6:16).

✦Most Mentioned Men (Answers)

1. Jesus.
2. David.
3. Moses.

4. What priest ranks fourth with a total of 339 references?

5. What king has one less reference than the answer to Question 4 and ranks fifth?

6. What patriarch, with 306 mentions, ranks seventh?

7. What wise king ranks eighth with his 295 mentions?

8. What man would, if his famous nickname were considered a real personal name, outrank all the others in this list? (As it stands, using his usual name, he ranks ninth with 270 mentions.)

9. What government leader in a foreign land ranks tenth with 208 references?

10. What military man ranks eleventh with 197 references?

11. What apostle ranks twelfth with 185 references?

12. What apostle ranks thirteenth with 166 references?

13. What military commander in the reign of David ranks fourteenth with 137 mentions?

14. What prophet ranks fifteenth and has only one less mention that the answer to Question 13?

15. What prophet and judge has only one less reference than the person in Question 14 and ranks sixteenth?

16. What patriarch, though he is mentioned much less than his father or son, ranks seventeenth with 127 mentions?

17. What kinsman of Jesus ranks eighteenth with 86 references?

18. What government official is, with 56 references, the most mentioned unbeliever in the New Testament?

19. How many times is Adam mentioned in the Bible?

20. After Peter and Paul, which apostle is mentioned the most times (35 references)?

4. Aaron.
5. Saul.
6. Abraham.
7. Solomon.
8. Jacob, whose name Israel occurs more than any other name in this list. However, the name is almost always used of the nation, not the man.
9. Joseph.
10. Joshua.
11. Paul.
12. Peter.
13. Joab.
14. Jeremiah.
15. Samuel.
16. Isaac.
17. John the Baptist.
18. Pilate.
19. Only 30.
20. John.

✦Most Mentioned Women

1. What Old Testament woman bore a child at age 90 and is the most mentioned woman in the Bible (56 mentions)?
2. What wife of a patriarch ranks second with 47 mentions?
3. What relative of Number 2 ranks third with 34 mentions?
4. What mother of twins ranks fourth with 31 mentions?
5. What evil woman ranks fifth with 23 mentions?
6. What New Testament woman ranks sixth with 19 mentions?
7. What wife of both Nabal and David ranks seventh with 15 mentions?
8. What sister of a famous leader ties with Number 7?
9. What follower of Jesus is mentioned 14 times?
10. What servant woman is also mentioned 14 times?
11. How many times is Eve, the first woman, mentioned?

✦Still More Kings, Pharaohs, and Other Rulers

1. Who built pagan temples to please all his foreign wives?
2. Which Gospel claims that Pilate had the plaque "The King of the Jews" fastened on Jesus' cross?
3. What Persian king was embarrassed by his disobedient wife?
4. What king of Judah was murdered after he fled to Lachish?
5. What king had a sinister prime minister named Haman?
6. What king is supposed to have written Ecclesiastes?

✦Most Mentioned Women (Answers)

1. Sarah.
2. Rachel.
3. Leah.
4. Rebekah.
5. Jezebel.
6. Mary, Jesus' mother.
7. Abigail.
8. Miriam.
9. Mary Magdalene.
10. Hagar.
11. Only 4.

✦Still More Kings, Pharaohs, and Other Rulers (Answers)

1. Solomon (1 Kings 11:1-13).
2. John (19:21).
3. Ahasuerus, or Xerxes (Esther 1:10-12).
4. Amaziah (2 Kings 14:19).
5. Ahasuerus, or Xerxes (Esther 3:1).
6. Solomon (Ecclesiastes 1:1).

7. What two kings are mentioned as the authors of Proverbs?

8. What future king of Israel was out hunting his donkeys when Samuel came to anoint him?

9. What much-loved and much-quoted prophet was active in the reigns of Uzziah, Jotham, Ahaz, and Hezekiah, and, according to tradition, was executed by Manasseh?

10. What king had the apostle James executed with a sword and had Peter arrested?

11. What fat king of Moab was murdered by the judge Ehud?

12. What king of Babylon went insane and lived in the fields, where he ate grass and let his hair and fingernails grow long?

13. What king made a famous judgment about a baby that two women claimed was theirs?

14. What king ordered Daniel thrown into the lions' den?

15. What king of Judah tore down the pagan shrines and stamped out child sacrifice in Judah?

16. What king of Judah sacrificed his sons in the fire but later became repentant?

17. What cruel king had the infant boys of Bethlehem slaughtered?

18. What king broke his own law when he called on a spiritualist to bring up the ghost of Samuel?

19. Who was the only king of Israel to kill both a king of Judah and a king of Israel?

20. What king was referred to by Jesus as "that fox"?

21. What son of Saul was made king of Israel by Abner?

22. What king executed John the Baptist after his wife's daughter asked for the head of John on a platter?

23. What Assyrian king attacked the Philistines, leading Isaiah to walk around naked for three years?

24. What king, dressed in royal finery, was hailed as a god but then struck down by the angel of the Lord?

25. What king did Paul tell the story of his conversion?

7. Solomon and Lemuel (Proverbs 1:1; 31:1).
8. Saul (1 Samuel 9:15—10:1).
9. Isaiah (1:1).
10. Herod Agrippa (Acts 12:1-3).
11. Eglon (Judges 3:15-30).
12. Nebuchadnezzar (Daniel 4:33).
13. Solomon (1 Kings 3:16-28).
14. Darius (Daniel 6).
15. Josiah (2 Kings 23:10-14).
16. Manasseh (2 Chronicles 33:1-17).
17. Herod (Matthew 2:16).
18. Saul (1 Samuel 28:3-19).
19. Jehu, who killed Jehoram and Ahaziah (2 Kings 9:24, 27).
20. Herod (Luke 13:31).
21. Ishbosheth (2 Samuel 2:10).
22. Herod (Mark 6:14-28).
23. Sargon (Isaiah 20).
24. Herod Agrippa (Acts 12:21-23).
25. Agrippa (Acts 26).

26. What king gave his daughter as a wife for David?
27. What Hebrew was given the daughter of the pharaoh as a wife?
28. According to Luke's Gospel, what Roman ruler ordered a census in the empire?
29. Who was the first king to reign at Jerusalem?
30. What saintly king of Judah was crippled with a foot disease in his old age?
31. What king was reprimanded by his military commander for weeping too long over his dead son?
32. What son of David tried to make himself king after David's death?
33. Who was king of Judah when the long-lost Book of the Law was found in the temple?
34. Who received a visit from the Queen of Sheba, whom he impressed with his wisdom?
35. Who is the only king who is said to have neither mother nor father?
36. What king of Judah became king at age seven and was aided in his reign by the saintly priest Jehoiada?
37. What king had the misfortune of his worst enemy being his son-in-law and the best friend of his son?
38. What king is considered to be the author of seventy-three of the Psalms?
39. What king built the first temple in Jerusalem?
40. What army commander made Saul's son Ishbosheth king over Israel?
41. What evil king of Israel pouted when he couldn't get a man to sell his plot of land?
42. What psalm is supposed to be David's expression of guilt after his affair with Bathsheba?
43. What king suffered from an almost fatal illness but was promised fifteen more years of life by Isaiah?
44. Which of the ten plagues finally convinced the Egyptian pharaoh to let the Israelites leave?
45. Who reigned in Persia when Nehemiah heard the sad news about the walls of Jerusalem?

26. Saul (1 Samuel 18:28).
27. Joseph (Genesis 41:45-46).
28. Caesar Augustus (Luke 2:1).
29. David (2 Samuel 5:9).
30. Asa (1 Kings 15:23).
31. David (2 Samuel 19:1-8).
32. Adonijah (1 Kings 1:5-53).
33. Josiah (2 Kings 22:8-10).
34. Solomon (1 Kings 10:1-13).
35. Melchizedek, king of Salem (Hebrews 7:3).
36. Joash (2 Kings 12:1-3).
37. Saul (1 Samuel 18:1, 28).
38. David.
39. Solomon (2 Chronicles 2:1).
40. Abner (2 Samuel 2:8-10).
41. Ahab (1 Kings 21:1-5).
42. Psalm 51.
43. Hezekiah (2 Kings 20:1-6).
44. The death of the firstborn (Exodus 12:30-32).
45. Artaxerxes (Nehemiah 1:1).

46. What king of Judah purified the temple and rededicated it to God?
47. What apostle fled the soldiers of King Aretas in Damascus?
48. What king of Israel was told by the prophet Jehu that the royal family would be wiped out because of its destruction of Jeroboam's dynasty?
49. What son of Solomon caused the kingdom to split when he threatened the people of Israel?
50. What king sent his son to David with expensive presents that David decided to use in worship?

✦A Herd of Prophets

1. This bald prophet was the performer of many miracles and the successor to another great prophet.
2. This court prophet confronted King David with his adultery.
3. This young prophet had a vision of a statue composed of different metals.
4. This prophet, put into a hole in the ground for being too outspoken, was often called the "weeping prophet."
5. This king of Israel was, early in his career, associated with a group of prophets.
6. This wilderness man confronted the prophets of Baal in a famous contest. He was taken to heaven in a chariot of fire.
7. This prophet, famous for his vision of the dry bones, was with the exiles in Babylon.
8. This prophet's work is quoted in the New Testament more than any other's. He is famous for his vision of God in the temple.
9. This kinsman of Jesus ate locusts, preached repentance, and baptized penitents in the Jordan.
10. This Christian prophesied a famine in the land.

46. Hezekiah (2 Chronicles 29).
47. Paul (2 Corinthians 11:32).
48. Baasha (1 Kings 16:1-4).
49. Rehoboam (1 Kings 12:1-17).
50. Toi, king of Hamath (2 Samuel 8:9-12).

✦A Herd of Prophets (Answers)

1. Elisha (1-2 Kings)
2. Nathan (2 Samuel, 1 Kings)
3. Daniel
4. Jeremiah
5. Saul (1 Samuel 10:1-13)
6. Elijah (1-2 Kings)
7. Ezekiel
8. Isaiah
9. John the Baptist
10. Agabus (Acts 11:27-28; 21:10-11)

11. This New Testament character prophesied the destruction of Jerusalem.
12. This woman was sent for when the long-neglected book of the law was found during Josiah's reign.
13. These four young women, daughters of a Christian evangelist, were considered prophetesses.
14. This elderly woman recognized the infant Jesus as being the Messiah.
15. This man, who anointed the first two kings of Israel, was considered both a judge and a prophet.
16. This prophet of Moab had a confrontation with his talking donkey.
17. This Old Testament patriarch was revealed as a prophet to King Abimelech.
18. This Egyptian-born Hebrew leader predicted the coming of a prophet like himself.
19. This prophet took David to task for numbering the people of Israel.
20. This prophet predicted that Jeroboam would be king over ten tribes of Israel.
21. This reluctant prophet was thrown overboard in a storm.
22. This man of Tekoa was a simple laborer who had the audacity to confront the king's priest at his shrine.
23. This man prophesied against Nineveh.
24. This prophet was famous for his marriage to a prostitute.
25. This prophet predicted the outpouring of God's Spirit upon all people.
26. This man wrote a brief book against Edom.
27. This sister of a Hebrew leader was herself a prophetess. For a time she was afflicted with leprosy.
28. The only female judge of Israel, this woman was considered a prophetess.
29. This apostle of Jesus recorded his visions of the world's end times.
30. This man, who traveled to Antioch with Paul, Silas, and Barnabas, was considered a prophet.

11. Jesus
12. Huldah (2 Kings 22)
13. The daughters of Philip (Acts 21:8-9)
14. Anna (Luke 2:36-38)
15. Samuel
16. Balaam (Numbers 22-24)
17. Abraham (Genesis 20:1-7)
18. Moses (Deuteronomy 18:15)
19. Gad (2 Samuel 24:10-14)
20. Ahijah (1 Kings 11:29-40)
21. Jonah
22. Amos
23. Nahum
24. Hosea
25. Joel
26. Obadiah
27. Miriam (Exodus 15:20)
28. Deborah (Judges 4:4)
29. John
30. Judas Barsabbas (Acts 15:22, 32)

31. This prophet spoke of the need to purify temple worship after the return from exile in Babylon. He spoke of the coming of someone like the prophet Elijah.

32. This man of Moresheth was a contemporary of Isaiah. He spoke of the need to walk humbly with God.

33. This prophet, who posed much of his book in the form of questions and answers, concluded that "the just shall live by faith."

34. Active during Josiah's reign, this prophet spoke about judgment and the coming "day of the Lord."

35. This unlucky prophet delivered an unfavorable message to King Ahab.

36. This false prophet wore a yoke, which Jeremiah broke.

37. This traveling companion of Paul was considered a prophet.

38. Active at the time of the rebuilding of the temple in Jerusalem, this prophet is associated with Zechariah.

39. This prophet, who lived in Jerusalem after the Babylonian exile, had visions of a flying scroll and a gold lampstand.

40. This man is spoken of as being his brother's prophet. He is also famous for having constructed a golden calf.

41. This false prophet wore iron horns and told King Ahab he would be victorious in battle.

42. This prophet told King Rehoboam that Judah would be abandoned to the forces of the Egyptian king.

43. This prophet, who lived in the reign of King Asa in Judah, was the son of the prophet Oded.

44. This false prophet was a sorcerer and an attendant of the proconsul, Sergius Paulus.

45. This prophetess is mentioned as an intimidator of Nehemiah.

46. This evil prophetess is referred to in Revelation by the name of an Old Testament queen.

31. Malachi
32. Micah
33. Habakkuk
34. Zephaniah
35. Micaiah ben-Imlah (1 Kings 22:8-28)
36. Hananiah (Jeremiah 28)
37. Silas (Acts 15:32)
38. Haggai
39. Zechariah
40. Aaron (Exodus 7:1)
41. Zedekiah (1 Kings 22:1-12)
42. Shemaiah (2 Chronicles 12:5-8)
43. Azariah (2 Chronicles 13:1-8)
44. Bar-Jesus (Acts 13:6-11)
45. Noadiah (Nehemiah 6:14)
46. Jezebel (Revelation 2:20)

✦Notable Women, and Some Less Notable (II)

1. Who was the mother of the Midianites?
2. What Gospel mentions Susanna, who had been healed by Jesus?
3. Who is the only Egyptian queen mentioned in the Bible?
4. What Egyptian woman found the infant Moses in the river?
5. What daughter of David was raped by her half brother?
6. What epistle mentions Tryphena, a faithful church worker?
7. Who was the wife of Haman of Persia?
8. Who were the first two women to hear that their husband had killed a man?
9. What servant woman of Leah's became the mother of two of the twelve tribes of Israel?
10. What were the names of Adam's daughters?
11. Whose daughters became the mothers of the Moabites and the Ammonites?
12. What priest of Midian had seven daughters, one of which became the wife of Moses?
13. What girl was offered as a sacrifice by her father, one of Israel's judges?
14. What daughter of a troublemaker married a Jewish priest, a marriage that caused him to lose his post?
16. What little girl was referred to as "Talitha" by Jesus?
17. What two Hebrew servant women risked their lives by disobeying the command of the pharaoh?
18. What harlot fled from a burning city, taking her family with her?
19. Whose ten concubines were forced to engage in public lewdness with the king's sons?
20. Who had an Israelite servant girl who told him about a cure for leprosy?

✦Notable Women, and Some Less Notable (II) (Answers)

1. Keturah, wife of Abraham (Genesis 25:1, 4).
2. Luke (8:3).
3. Tahpenes (1 Kings 11:19).
4. Pharaoh's daughter (Exodus 2:5).
5. Tamar (2 Samuel 13).
6. Romans (16:12).
7. Zeresh (Esther 5:10).
8. Zilah and Adah, wives of Lamech (Genesis 4:19-23).
9. Zilpah, mother of Asher and Gad (Genesis 30:11-13).
10. They are not named.
11. Lot's (Genesis 19:30-38).
12. Jethro, or Reuel (Exodus 2:16-20).
13. Jephthah's daughter (Judges 11).
14. The daughter of Sanballat, and wife of Joiada (Nehemiah 13:28).
15. Jairus' daughter (Matthew 9:18-25).
17. Puah and Shiprah (Exodus 1:15).
18. Rahab (Joshua 6:25).
19. David's (2 Samuel 15:16; 16:22; 20:3).
20. Naaman (2 Kings 5:2).

21. Who urged her husband to curse God and die?
22. What apostle had a sister whose son informed soldiers of a murderous plot?
23. Who was forbidden to mourn the death of his beautiful wife?
24. What invading general had a loving mother who never saw her son return from battle?
25. What woman in the time of the judges had dedicated 1,100 shekels of silver to the making of idols?
26. Whose mother took refuge in Moab while her son was fleeing the wrath of Israel's king?
27. What woman put on an act to convince David to recall Absalom from exile?
28. What was the occupation of the two women who disputed over a child and asked Solomon for a decision?
29. What city suffered such a terrible famine that two women agreed to eat their sons for dinner?
30. What woman is mentioned in Proverbs as having taught wise sayings to her son?
31. What book portrays Wisdom as a woman?
32. What grief stricken woman turned away from her diseased husband because his breath was so offensive?
33. Where did the faithful mother of Rufus live?
34. What violent son of Gideon was killed by a woman who dropped a millstone on his skull?
35. Who tricked his enemies by leaving a harlot's house earlier than expected?
36. Who is the only woman in the Bible described as a "wench"?
37. Who helped David by hiding two of his messengers in her cistern?
38. What woman saved her city by negotiating peacefully with Joab?
39. What prophet pictures women weeping for the god Tammuz?

21. Job's wife (Job 2:9).
22. Paul (Acts 23:16).
23. Ezekiel (24:16-18).
24. Sisera's mother (Judges 5:28).
25. Micah's mother (Judges 17:2-4).
26. David's (1 Samuel 22:3-4).
27. The wise woman of Tekoa (2 Samuel 14).
28. Harlots (1 Kings 3:16-28).
29. Samaria (2 Kings 6:20, 26-30).
30. King Lemuel's mother (Proverbs 31:1).
31. Proverbs (chapter 8).
32. Job's wife (Job 19:17).
33. Rome (Romans 16:13).
34. Abimelech (Judges 9:53).
35. Samson (Judges 16:1-3).
36. The woman of En-rogel who acted as a liaison between David and the high priest (2 Samuel 17:17).
37. The Bahurim woman (2 Samuel 17:19).
38. The wise woman of Abel (2 Samuel 20:16-22).
39. Ezekiel (8:14).

40. Who is the first female barber mentioned in the Bible?

41. Where did Paul exorcise a spirit from a girl who later became a believer?

42. Which epistle mentions "silly women" who are always learning but never aware of the truth?

43. Which epistle is addressed to a woman?

44. How many times does Eve's name appear in Genesis?

45. How many times does Eve's name appear in the New Testament?

46. Which Gospel records Jesus saying, "Remember Lot's wife"?

47. What shepherd girl became the much-loved wife of Jacob?

48. What daughter of Jacob caused major problems by venturing into strange territory?

49. What quick-witted widow secured children through her deceived father-in-law?

50. What Egyptian wife caused Joseph to be thrown into prison?

51. What Midianite woman married Moses?

52. What Moabite was an ancestor of Jesus?

53. Who is the first female singer mentioned in the Bible?

54. What woman was married to a fool with a name that meant "fool"?

55. What singer was shut out of the Israelite camp for seven days when she was stricken with leprosy?

56. What five women demanded that Moses give them their deceased father's estate, though women had no property rights at the time?

57. What woman of Jericho was spared when Joshua's men took the city?

58. What unfortunate woman was gang-raped, then cut into twelve pieces and sent to the tribes of Israel?

59. Who brought down Samson for the price of 1,100 pieces of silver from each of the Philistine chieftains?

40. Delilah (Judges 16:19).
41. Philippi (Acts 16:16).
42. 2 Timothy (3:6-7).
43. 2 John.
44. Twice (Genesis 3:20; 4:1).
45. Twice (2 Corinthians 11:3; 1 Timothy 2:13).
46. Luke (17:32).
47. Rachel (Genesis 29:6).
48. Dinah (Genesis 34).
49. Tamar (Genesis 38).
50. The wife of Potiphar (Genesis 39:7-20).
51. Zipporah (Exodus 2:21).
52. Ruth (4:17).
53. Miriam (Exodus 15:21).
54. Abigail (1 Samuel 25:23-25).
55. Miriam (Numbers 12).
56. The five daughters of Zelophehad (Numbers 26–27).
57. Rahab (Joshua 6:17).
58. The Levite's concubine (Judges 19–20).
59. Delilah (Judges 16:5).

60. At whose house did Peter confront maids who asked him if he was one of Jesus' disciples?

61. What famous Moabite woman was married to Chilion of Israel?

62. Who was the Kate Smith of the Hebrews?

63. What woman was suspected of drunkenness as she prayed in the sanctuary at Shiloh?

64. Who was David's first wife?

65. What young girl was brought in to warm the cold bones of old King David?

66. What name was borne by one of David's wives and one of his mothers-in-law?

67. Who was stricken with leprosy for speaking out against her brother?

68. What famous woman judge was married to the obscure man named Lapidoth?

69. What was Moses' mother's name?

70. What woman gave up her son to the household of an Egyptian but came to raise him in her own home anyway?

71. What Midianite woman was the daughter of a priest and the wife of a former Egyptian prince?

72. What woman of dubious character hid Israelite spies under piles of flax?

73. What woman from an idol-worshiping nation became an ancestor of Christ?

74. What barren woman begged the Lord for a son, and later gave up her only son to live in the house of the priest Eli?

75. Who took great pains to make peace between David and her foolish and obnoxious husband?

76. What unnamed woman broke the king's law by order of the king himself?

77. What wife of David took enormous pains to secure the throne for her son?

78. What son of David was always referred to as the "son of Haggith"?

60. The high priest's (Matthew 26:69-71; Mark 14:66-69).
61. Ruth (1:2-5).
62. Miriam, who sang a patriotic song after the crossing of the Red Sea (Exodus 15:21).
63. Hannah (1 Samuel 1:13-14).
64. Michal (1 Samuel 18:27).
65. Abishag (1 Kings 1:3, 15).
66. Ahinoam (1 Samuel 14:50; 25:43).
67. Miriam (Numbers 12).
68. Deborah (Judges 4:4).
69. Jochebed (Exodus 6:20).
70. Jochebed, Moses' mother (Exodus 2:8-10).
71. Zipporah, Moses' wife (Exodus 2:21).
72. Rahab (Joshua 2:6).
73. Ruth (4:17).
74. Hannah (1 Samuel 1:20-25).
75. Abigail (1 Samuel 25:23-35).
76. The witch of Endor (1 Samuel 28:7-25).
77. Bathsheba, mother of Solomon (1 Kings 1).
78. Adonijah (1 Kings 1:11).

79. What wife of David is mentioned in Matthew's genealogy of Jesus?
80. Who came to Jesus at the wedding of Cana and said, "They have no wine"?
81. What queen of Israel ordered the extermination of the prophets of the Lord?
82. Who was killed after being thrown from a window by two eunuchs?
83. What woman, associated with the prophet Elijah, was mentioned by Jesus?
84. What wealthy woman had a son that died of sunstroke?
85. What daughter of Jezebel was killed at Jerusalem's Horse Gate?
86. What wise woman was sought out by Josiah when the Book of the Law was discovered in the temple?
87. What book of the Bible mentions a virtuous woman who is more valuable than rubies?
88. Who was the first woman to ask the Lord for help?
89. Who was Jesus speaking of when he said, "Behold your mother"?
90. What servant of David was desired as a prize by his son Adonijah?

✦The Inventors

1. Who was the first person to practice wine-making?
2. What righteous man started the practice of herding sheep?
3. What mighty man was the first hunter?
4. Who invented farming?
5. Who invented the art of working with metal?
6. Who was the first man to build a city?
7. Who invented music-making?
8. Who invented tents?

79. Bathsheba (Matthew 1:6).
80. Mary (John 2:3).
81. Jezebel (1 Kings 18:4).
82. Jezebel (2 Kings 9:33).
83. The widow of Zarephath (Luke 4:25-26).
84. The woman of Shunam (2 Kings 4:19).
85. Athaliah (2 Chronicles 23:14).
86. Huldah the prophetess (2 Kings 22:14).
87. Proverbs (31:10-31).
88. Rebekah (Genesis 25:22).
89. Mary (John 19:27).
90. Abishag, the Shunammite (1 Kings 2:17).

✦The Inventors (Answers)

1. Noah (Genesis 9:20-21).
2. Abel (Genesis 4:2).
3. Nimrod (Genesis 10:8-9).
4. Cain (Genesis 4:2).
5. Tubal-Cain (Genesis 4:22).
6. Cain (Genesis 4:17).
7. Jubal, inventor of the harp and organ (Genesis 4:21).
8. Jabal (Genesis 4:20).

✦Down on the Farm

1. What was the farmer Elisha doing when Elijah threw his mantle upon him?
2. What suffering man was a farmer?
3. Who planted the first garden?
4. What judge was a wheat farmer?
5. What king of Judah loved farming?
6. Who was the first man to plant a vineyard?
7. What barley farmer married a Moabite woman and became an ancestor of David?
8. Who was the first farmer?
9. For what cripple did David order Ziba to farm the land?
10. Who had a vineyard that Ahab coveted?
11. What patriarch farmed in Gerar and received a hundredfold harvest?
12. What lieutenant of David had his barley fields destroyed by Absalom?
13. What king, famous for his building projects, also planted vineyards, gardens, and orchards?

✦Late-night Callers

1. Who came to Peter late at night and released him from prison?
2. Who had a late-night visit from an angel, who assured him that he would be safe aboard a storm-tossed ship?
3. Who led some officers of the chief priests to pay a late-night call on Jesus?
4. What Pharisee came to Jesus late at night?
5. Who met a man with whom he engaged in an all-night wrestling match?
6. Who came through Egypt on a late-night visit to almost every household?

✦Down on the Farm (Answers)

1. Plowing (1 Kings 19:19).
2. Job (1:14).
3. God (Genesis 2:8).
4. Gideon (Judges 6:11).
5. Uzziah (2 Chronicles 26:9-10).
6. Noah (Genesis 9:20).
7. Boaz (Ruth 1:22—2:3).
8. Cain (Genesis 4:2).
9. Mephibosheth, Saul's grandson (2 Samuel 9:9-10).
10. Naboth (1 Kings 21:1-2).
11. Isaac (Genesis 26:12).
12. Joab (2 Samuel 14:30).
13. Solomon (Ecclesiastes 2:4-5).

✦Late-night Callers (Answers)

1. An angel (Acts 12:6-17).
2. Paul (Acts 27:23-24).
3. Judas (John 18:3, 12).
4. Nicodemus (John 3:1-2).
5. Jacob (Genesis 32:22-31).
6. The angel of death (Exodus 12:29-31).

7. Where did shepherds receive angels as late visitors?
8. Who took Saul's spear after sneaking into his camp late one night?
9. Who visited a medium at night?
10. Who attacked a Midianite camp late at night?
11. Who paid the young Samuel a late-night call?
12. Who frightened his followers, who thought he was a ghost when he passed by them late at night?

✦They Heard Voices

1. What New Testament character was the "voice crying in the wilderness"?
2. What blind father recognized Jacob's voice but was deceived by his glove-covered hands?
3. When Moses was in the tabernacle, where did God's voice come from?
4. Who heard a voice that said, "Write down what you see"?
5. Where did God speak to Moses in a voice like thunder?
6. What barren woman moved her lips in prayer but made no sound?
7. According to Deuteronomy, where did God's voice come from?
8. Who told Saul that obeying God's voice was more important than sacrificing animals?
9. Which Gospel mentions the voice of Rachel weeping for her children?
10. Who heard the voice of an angel ordering that a large tree be chopped down?
11. What book says that the divine voice sounds like a waterfall?
12. Who said, "Is that your voice, David my son"?
13. To which church did Jesus say, "If any man hear my voice, and open the door, I will come in to him"?

7. Near Bethlehem (Luke 2:8-16).
8. David and Abishai (1 Samuel 26:7-12).
9. Saul (1 Samuel 28:8).
10. Gideon and his men (Judges 7:19).
11. The Lord (1 Samuel 4:1-14).
12. Jesus, when he walked on the lake (Mark 6:48).

✦They Heard Voices (Answers)

1. John the Baptist (Mark 1:3).
2. Isaac (Genesis 27:22).
3. Above the ark of the covenant (Numbers 7:89).
4. John (Revelation 1:10).
5. Mount Sinai (Exodus 19:19).
6. Hannah (1 Samuel 1:13).
7. The fire (Deuteronomy 5:24).
8. Samuel (1 Samuel 15:22).
9. Matthew (2:18).
10. Daniel (4:14).
11. Revelation (1:15).
12. Saul (1 Samuel 26:17).
13. Laodicea (Revelation 3:20).

14. What apostle addressed the Pentecost crowd in a loud voice?

15. Who cried out at the top of her voice when she saw Samuel raised from the dead?

16. At what event did a voice from heaven say, "This is my beloved Son, in whom I am well pleased"?

17. What boy was sleeping near the ark of the covenant when he heard God's voice calling to him?

18. Where was Jesus when the divine voice said, "This is my beloved Son . . . hear ye him"?

19. What king heard the voice of God in the temple—although there was no temple at the time?

20. Who heard the voice of those who had been killed for proclaiming God's word?

21. Who heard God's voice after running away from Queen Jezebel?

22. Who screamed in a loud voice, asking Jesus not to punish him?

23. What king was told by Isaiah that the king of Assyria had raised his voice up against God?

24. What was the problem of the ten men who called to Jesus in a loud voice, begging him for mercy?

25. Who heard the "still, small voice" of God?

26. What criminal did the people of Jerusalem cry out in a loud voice for?

27. Who heard God speaking out of a whirlwind?

28. What bird did John hear crying in a loud voice, "Woe, woe to the inhabiters of the earth"?

29. According to Psalm 19, what has a voice that goes out to all the world?

30. Who said that the bridegroom's friend is happy when he hears the bridegroom's voice?

31. According to Psalms, what trees are broken by the power of God's voice?

32. Who heard a voice telling of the fall of Babylon?

33. Which Gospel mentions the dead awakening to the voice of the Son of God?

14. Peter (Acts 2:14).
15. The witch of Endor (1 Samuel 28:12).
16. Jesus' baptism (Matthew 3:17).
17. Samuel (1 Samuel 3:3-14).
18. On the Mount of Transfiguration (Matthew 17:5).
19. David (2 Samuel 22:7).
20. John (Revelation 6:10).
21. Elijah (1 Kings 19:13).
22. The Gerasene demoniac (Mark 5:7).
23. Hezekiah (2 Kings 19:22).
24. Leprosy (Luke 17:13).
25. Elijah (1 Kings 19:12).
26. Barabbas (Luke 23:18).
27. Job (38:1).
28. An eagle (Revelation 8:13).
29. The heavens (Psalm 19:4).
30. John the Baptist (John 3:29).
31. The cedars of Lebanon (Psalm 29:5).
32. John (Revelation 18:2).
33. John (5:25).

34. What, according to Proverbs, lifts its voice up in the streets?

35. What city in Revelation was seen as a place that would never again hear the voices of brides and grooms?

36. According to Jesus, whose voice do the sheep know?

37. What book mentions the sweet voices of lovers in the garden?

38. In Revelation, where did the voice proclaiming the new heaven and earth come from?

39. Who heard God's voice in the temple in the year that King Uzziah died?

40. Who came forth when Jesus called to him in a loud voice?

41. What prophet predicted that Rachel's voice would be heard, wailing for her dead children?

42. Which Gospel mentions the voice of God speaking during Jesus' farewell address to his disciples?

43. What prophet mentions Jerusalem with the voice of a ghost?

44. Who heard the voice of Jesus many months after Jesus' ascension to heaven?

45. What epistle mentions an archangel's voice in connection with the resurrection of believers?

46. What prophet's voice did the returned Jewish exiles obey?

47. What prophet mentions a voice crying in the wilderness?

48. Who heard the divine voice telling him to eat unclean animals?

49. What king heard God's voice just as he was boasting about how great Babylon was?

50. Who heard the voice of God as he watched four mysterious creatures flying under a crystal dome?

51. Who recognized Peter's voice after he was miraculously delivered from prison?

52. According to Isaiah, what noble person will not lift up his voice in the streets?

34. Wisdom (Proverbs 1:20).
35. Babylon (Revelation 18:23).
36. The shepherd's (John 10:4).
37. Song of Solomon (2:14, 8:13).
38. The throne (Revelation 21:3).
39. Isaiah (6:8).
40. Lazarus (John 11:43).
41. Jeremiah (31:15).
42. John (12:28-30).
43. Isaiah (29:4).
44. Paul (Acts 9:4).
45. 1 Thessalonians (4:16).
46. Haggai's (1:12).
47. Isaiah (40:3).
48. Peter (Acts 10:13-15).
49. Nebuchadnezzar (Daniel 4:31).
50. Ezekiel (1:24).
51. Rhoda (Acts 12:14).
52. The Lord's servant (Isaiah 42:2).

53. According to Paul, what language did the divine voice use on the Damascus road?
54. What king called to Daniel in an anguished voice?
55. Which epistle mentions the voice of Balaam's donkey?

◆Teacher, Teacher

1. What famous rabbi was Paul's teacher?
2. Who commissioned Ezra to teach the law to Israel?
3. According to Jesus, who would teach his followers all they needed to know?
4. What two men were to instruct the people involved in the construction of the tabernacle?
5. What king of Judah sent his princes throughout the land to teach the law to the people?
6. What learned Greek taught in the synagogue at Ephesus but was himself instructed by Aquila and Priscilla?
7. What king sent an exiled priest back to Samaria to teach the Gentiles there how to follow God?
8. What apostle taught and disputed in the lecture hall of a man named Tyrannus?
9. Who was supposed to teach the Israelites how to deal with lepers?
10. What New Testament word means "teacher"?

◆Sleepers and Non-sleepers

1. Who had surgery performed on him as he slept?
2. Who was killed as he slept in the tent of Jael?
3. Who slept in the bottom of a ship as it rolled in a storm?

53. Hebrew (or, in some translations, Aramaic) (Acts 26:14).
54. Darius (Daniel 6:20).
55. 2 Peter (2:16).

✦Teacher, Teacher (Answers)

1. Gamaliel (Acts 22:3).
2. King Artaxerxes (Ezra 7:25).
3. The Comforter (John 14:26).
4. Bezaleel and Aholiab (Exodus 35:30-35).
5. Jehoshaphat (2 Chronicles 17:7-9).
6. Apollos (Acts 18:24-26).
7. The king of Assyria (2 Kings 17:28).
8. Paul (Acts 19:9).
9. The priests (Deuteronomy 24:8).
10. Rabbi (John 1:38).

✦Sleepers and Non-sleepers (Answers)

1. Adam (Genesis 2:21).
2. Sisera (Judges 4:21).
3. Jonah (1:5).

4. Who suggested to Jezebel's priests that Baal was sleeping on duty?
5. Who slept at Bethel and dreamed about angels?
6. Who slept at David's door while he was home on furlough?
7. Who could not sleep on the night after Haman built a gallows for hanging Mordecai?
8. Who had troublesome dreams that kept him from sleeping?
9. Who was visited by an angel of the Lord while sleeping?
10. Who slept while Jesus prayed in Gethsemane?
11. Who sneaked into Saul's camp while he was asleep?
12. Who spoke to Abram while he was in a deep sleep?
13. Who did not sleep while Daniel was in the lions' den?
14. Who slept through a haircut?
15. Who slept during a storm on the Sea of Galilee?
16. Who fell asleep during Paul's sermon and was later raised by Paul?
17. Who was sleeping between two soldiers when an angel came to release him?
18. Who was awakened from a deep sleep by an earthquake that toppled a prison?
19. According to Jesus, this person was not dead, but only sleeping. Who was it?
20. Who told Laban he had gone twenty years without a decent sleep?
21. According to Proverbs, what does it take for the wicked to sleep well?
22. Which epistle tells sleepers to rise from the dead?
23. Which epistle uses sleep as a metaphor for physical death?
24. What boy was called out of his sleep by the voice of God?
25. Which epistle urges believers to be alert, not asleep?
26. Who was in a deep sleep as the angel Gabriel explained a vision?

4. Elijah (1 Kings 18:27).
 5. Jacob (Genesis 28:11-15).
 6. Uriah (2 Samuel 11:9).
 7. King Ahasuerus (Esther 6:1).
 8. Nebuchadnezzar (Daniel 2:1).
 9. Joseph (Matthew 2:13).
10. The disciples (Luke 22:45).
11. David and Abishai (1 Samuel 26:7).
12. God (Genesis 15:12-16).
13. King Darius (Daniel 6:18).
14. Samson (Judges 16:19).
15. Jesus (Luke 8:23-24).
16. Eutychus (Acts 20:9-12).
17. Peter (Acts 12:6-7).
18. The Philippian jailor (Acts 16:27).
19. Jairus's daughter (Luke 8:52).
20. Jacob (Genesis 31:38, 40).
21. Causing trouble (Proverbs 4:16).
22. Ephesians (5:14).
23. 1 Corinthians 15.
24. Samuel (1 Samuel 3:2-10).
25. 1 Thessalonians (5:4-8).
26. Daniel (8:15-18).

✦Godly Government Workers in Ungodly Places

1. What Hebrew governed Egypt?
2. What upright young man was made ruler over the whole province of Babylon?
3. What island was Sergius Paulus, who became a Christian, the deputy of?
4. What Persian king did Nehemiah serve under?
5. What church in Greece had believers that were workers in "Caesar's household"?
6. From what country was the eunuch that was baptized by Philip?
7. What Jewish man served as an honored official under Ahasuerus of Persia?
8. What Roman centurion of Caesarea was a godly man?
9. What three Hebrew men were appointed Babylonian administrators by Nebuchadnezzar?
10. What was the occupation of the Roman who had his beloved servant healed by Jesus?
11. What Jewish girl became queen of Persia?

✦Notable Women, and Some Less Notable (III)

1. What New Testament woman was married to a priest named Zacharias?
2. Who begged her sister for some mandrakes, hoping they would help her bear children?
3. To what woman did Jesus declare, "I am the resurrection and the life"?
4. Who sat at Jesus' feet while her sister kept house?
5. What two women witnessed Jesus' tears over their dead brother?

✦Godly Government Workers in Ungodly Places (Answers)

1. Joseph (Genesis 42:6).
2. Daniel (2:48).
3. Cyprus (Acts 13:4-7).
4. Artaxerxes (Nehemiah 1:11).
5. Philippi (Philippians 4:22).
6. Ethiopia (Acts 8:27).
7. Mordecai (Esther 10:3).
8. Cornelius (Acts 10:1-2).
9. Shadrach, Meshach, and Abednego (Daniel 2:49).
10. A centurion (Luke 7:2-10).
11. Esther (2:17).

✦Notable Women, and Some Less Notable (III) (Answers)

1. Elisabeth (Luke 1:5).
2. Rachel (Genesis 30:14).
3. Martha (John 11:24-26).
4. Mary (Luke 10:39-42).
5. Mary and Martha (John 11:32-39).

6. What disciple's mother-in-law was healed of a fever by Jesus?
7. What wicked woman, the wife of a wicked king, brought about the death of John the Baptist?
8. How long did cousins Mary and Elisabeth spend together during their pregnancies?
9. Who offered to bear the guilt if her scheme to deceive her aged husband was found out?
10. Who said to her husband, "Give me children, or else I die"?
11. Which of Jacob's wives was the first to bear children?
12. What woman was called a prophetess by Luke?
13. Who died in giving birth to Benjamin?
14. What clever woman hoodwinked her father-in-law out of a signet ring and bracelets?
15. Who falsely accused her Hebrew servant of trying to seduce her?
16. What woman was the mother of two of Jesus' disciples?
17. Who asked Jesus for the special water that would quench her thirst forever?
18. Who called Jesus "Rabboni"?
19. To what earthy woman did Jesus say, "God is a spirit"?
20. Which of David's wives was described as "very beautiful to look upon"?
21. What wife, seeing her husband on the verge of death, circumcised their son?
22. Who criticized her famous brother for being married to an Ethiopian woman?
23. What Old Testament woman is mentioned in the roll of the faithful in Hebrews 11?
24. What woman gave needed courage to the fainthearted military man Barak?
25. Who pouted when her strongman lover kept fooling her about the source of his strength?

6. Peter's (Mark 1:30-31).
7. Herodias, wife of Herod (Luke 3:19).
8. Three months (Luke 1:56).
9. Rebekah (Genesis 27:13).
10. Rachel (Genesis 30:1).
11. Leah (Genesis 29:31).
12. Anna (Luke 2:36).
13. Rachel (Genesis 35:18).
14. Tamar (Genesis 38:17).
15. Potiphar's wife (Genesis 39:14).
16. Salome (Mark 15:40). While this verse does not specifically say that Salome is the mother of James and John, Matthew 27:56 mentions that two Marys and the mother of James and John were watching the crucifixion, so we may assume from Matthew and Mark that the third woman, Salome, was the mother of James and John.
17. The Samaritan woman (John 4:15).
18. Mary Magdalene (John 20:16).
19. The Samaritan woman (John 4:24).
20. Bathsheba, or Bath-shua (2 Samuel 11:2).
21. Zipporah (Exodus 4:25).
22. Miriam (Numbers 12:1).
23. Rahab (Hebrews 11:31).
24. Deborah (Judges 4:8).
25. Delilah (Judges 16).

26. Who lay down at her future husband's feet and was accepted by him?
27. Which of David's wives "despised him in her heart"?
28. What wife of a sheepherder admitted that her husband was a complete fool?
29. Who killed a fatted calf and made bread for a despairing king?
30. Who was the mother of John Mark?
31. Who was the royal mother of Nathan, Shobab, and Shimea?
32. Who came to Jerusalem with a caravan of camels and loads of jewels?
33. Who ran to tell people that she had met the Christ by a well?
34. What woman set up a special apartment for the prophet Elisha?
35. What book mentions an industrious woman who plants a vineyard with her own hands?
36. Who was the angel Gabriel speaking to when he said, "Blessed art thou among women"?
37. Where was Mary the last time she is mentioned in the New Testament?
38. Who was the first woman to tell Jesus she believed he was the Messiah?
39. What was the affliction of the woman who touched the hem of Jesus' robe?
40. To whom did Jesus say, "I am not sent but unto the lost sheep of the house of Israel"?
41. Who asked that her two sons could have places of priority in Jesus' kingdom?
42. What woman had had five husbands and was living with another man?
43. What woman accused Elijah of murdering her son, a son that Elijah then raised from the dead?
44. What woman had been healed of seven demons by Jesus?
45. How many Marys are in the New Testament?

26. Ruth (3:4-9).
27. Michal (2 Samuel 6:16).
28. Abigail (1 Samuel 25:25).
29. The witch of Endor (1 Samuel 28:24).
30. Mary (Acts 12:12).
31. Bathsheba (1 Chronicles 3:5).
32. The queen of Sheba (1 Kings 10:2).
33. The Samaritan woman (John 4:29).
34. The woman of Shunam (2 Kings 4:9).
35. Proverbs (31:16).
36. Mary (Luke 1:28).
37. With the apostles in the upper room in Jerusalem
    (Acts 1:13-14).
38. Martha (John 11:24-27).
39. An issue of blood (Mark 5:31).
40. The Syro-Phoenician woman of Canaan (Matthew 15:24).
41. The mother of John and James (Matthew 20:21).
42. The Samaritan woman (John 4:18).
43. The widow of Zarephath (1 Kings 17:18).
44. Mary Magdalene (Mark 16:9).
45. Six—Jesus' mother, Mary of Bethany, Mary Magdalene, Mary
    mother of James and Joses, Mary mother of John Mark, and
    Mary of Rome.

46. Who was the first woman to go against Jesus' words "You cannot serve God and mammon"?
47. What woman had Tabitha as a pet name?
48. What woman had the same name as an old kingdom of Asia?
49. What daughter of Job had a twelve-letter name?
50. What woman was capable enough to instruct the brilliant Apollos in theology?
51. Who was probably the carrier of Paul's epistle to the Romans?
52. What pastor was the son of the devout Eunice?
53. Who was with David when Bathsheba and Nathan pleaded with him to designate Solomon as his successor?
54. Who was given by her Egyptian father as a reward to a Hebrew servant?
55. What evil woman lived in the Valley of Sorek?
56. Who was Timothy's devout grandmother?
57. What woman, wife of the wicked king Amon, gave birth to the future godly king Josiah?
58. What courageous woman risked her life to keep her royal nephew alive?
59. What Jewish Christian woman had lived at Rome, Corinth, and Ephesus?
60. Who called herself Marah, a name meaning "bitter"?
61. Who asked her royal son to surrender his father's concubine to another son?
62. What wealthy woman made her living selling purple dye?
63. What woman had such an influential life that Israel had forty years of peace?
64. Who was better to her widowed mother-in-law than any seven sons could be?
65. Who bore three sons and two daughters after giving up her first son to serve the Lord at Shiloh?
66. What wife of David had no children because she had criticized her husband's jubilant dancing?

46. Sapphira, wife of Ananias (Acts 5).
47. Dorcas (Acts 9:36, 39).
48. Lydia (Acts 16:14).
49. Keren-happuch (42:14).
50. Priscilla (Acts 18:26).
51. Phoebe (Romans 16:1-2).
52. Timothy (2 Timothy 1:5).
53. Abishag (1 Kings 1:15).
54. Asenath, wife of Joseph (Genesis 41:45).
55. Delilah (Judges 16:4).
56. Lois (2 Timothy 1:5).
57. Jedidah (2 Kings 22:1).
58. Jehosheba, Joash's aunt (2 Kings 11:2-3).
59. Priscilla (Acts 18:2, 18, 24-26).
60. Naomi (Ruth 1:19-21).
61. Bathsheba (1 Kings 2:20).
62. Lydia (Acts 16:14).
63. Deborah (Judges 5:31).
64. Ruth (4:15).
65. Hannah (1 Samuel 2:21).
66. Michal (2 Samuel 6:23).

67. Who married David after her stupid husband died out of fear?

68. Who was the last woman to have dinner with King Saul?

69. Who was the first woman to be ashamed of her clothing?

70. Who was given a miraculous supply of food by the prophet Elijah?

71. What faithful woman did Elisha warn of a coming famine?

72. Who said, "Thy father and I have sought thee sorrowing"?

73. Who referred to Mary as the "mother of my Lord"?

74. What New Testament woman holds the record for widowhood—eighty-four years?

75. Who anointed Jesus' feet with precious ointment?

76. Who had her conversation with Jesus interrupted by his disciples, who criticized him for speaking with a woman?

77. Who was the first woman to see Jesus' empty tomb?

78. What two tribes of Israel were descended from an Egyptian woman?

79. What pagan woman of the Gospels is traditionally identified with the Christian woman Claudia mentioned in 2 Timothy?

80. What Christian woman was noted for helping the poor in the early church?

81. What woman, once possessed by demons, was the first to see the risen Christ?

82. What woman's absence made the Israelites pause in their journey to the promised land?

83. What woman was the first Christian convert in Europe?

84. What woman has been proposed as the author of the Epistle to the Hebrews?

85. What devout woman was described by Paul as "our sister" and "a servant of the church"?

67. Abigail (1 Samuel 25:36-42).
68. The witch of Endor (1 Samuel 28:25).
69. Eve—actually, she was ashamed of her lack of clothing (Genesis 3:7).
70. The widow of Zarephath (1 Kings 17:16).
71. The woman of Shunem (2 Kings 8:1).
72. Mary (Luke 2:48).
73. Elisabeth (Luke 1:41-43).
74. Anna (Luke 2:36-37).
75. Mary of Bethany (John 12:3).
76. The Samaritan woman (John 4:27).
77. Mary Magdalene (John 20:1).
78. Manasseh and Ephraim—their father Joseph was married to Asenath of Egypt (Genesis 41:50-52).
79. Pilate's wife.
80. Dorcas (Acts 9:36, 39).
81. Mary Magdalene (John 20:14).
82. Miriam's (Numbers 12:15).
83. Lydia (Acts 16:14).
84. Priscilla.
85. Phoebe (Romans 16:1-2).

86. What book features a dark Shulamite woman who sings to her loved one?

87. In the ridiculous riddle of the Sadducees, how many husbands did the hypothetical woman have?

88. What was the proposed punishment for the woman taken in adultery, later forgiven by Jesus?

89. Where was Paul when he cast demons out from a girl who was a spiritualist?

90. What was the hometown of Mary and Martha and Lazarus?

91. What beautiful woman of Israel was married to a Hittite warrior?

92. What distraught woman failed at first to recognize the resurrected Jesus?

93. What doting mother made her absentee a new coat each year?

94. What book speaks of the "sons of God" taking the "daughters of men" as wives?

95. What woman is significant for keeping her own name when she married instead of taking her husband's name?

96. Who had ten concubines that were sexually assaulted by his wayward son?

97. What book has a chorus of girls of Jerusalem as characters?

◆Not to Be Taken Seriously (I)

1. Why was Moses the most wicked man?

2. What book of the Bible mentions a baseball player who hit ten home runs?

3. What Old Testament character must have been as strong as steel?

4. How long was Noah in the belly of the whale?

5. How do we know there were newspaper reporters in Bible times?

86. The Song of Solomon.
87. Seven (Mark 12:20-25).
88. Stoning (John 8:3-11).
89. Philippi (Acts 16:16).
90. Bethany (John 11:1).
91. Bathsheba, wife of Uriah (2 Samuel 11:3).
92. Mary Magdalene (John 20:14-15).
93. Hannah (1 Samuel 2:19).
94. Genesis (6:2).
95. The daughter of Barzillai (Ezra 2:61).
96. David (2 Samuel 16:21-22).
97. The Song of Solomon.

✦Not to Be Taken Seriously (I) (Answers)

1. He broke all Ten Commandments at once (Exodus 32:15-19).
2. Numbers 11:32—"He that gathered least gathered ten homers."
3. Iron (Joshua 19:38).
4. Noah wasn't in the belly of the whale—Jonah was.
5. Zacchaeus couldn't see Jesus for the press (Luke 19:3).

6. Out of Gideon's seventy sons, how many were big men at birth?
7. What kind of lights did Noah use on the ark?
8. How does a lawyer resemble a rabbi?
9. What character was the most ambitious man?
10. Who was the greatest speaker?
11. Who had his seat in a theater changed?
12. Who was the first canning factory run by?
13. Why was Noah like a hungry cat?
14. What is it that Adam never saw or had, yet left two of them for his children?
15. What Bible character may have only been a foot tall?
16. What did Joseph in the Old Testament have in common with Zacchaeus in the New?
17. What did Jesus have in common with the fish that swallowed Jonah?
18. How do we know Isaiah's parents were good business people?
19. What kind of fur did Adam and Eve wear?
20. If Moses had dropped his rod in the Nile, what would it have become?
21. Since Methuselah was the oldest man in the Bible, why did he die before his father?
22. During what season did Eve eat the forbidden fruit?
23. What king mutilated sports equipment?
24. Who was the Bible's straightest man?
25. Why did poor Job land in bed with a cold?
26. Who was the first person to eat herself out of house and home?
27. What is the difference between Noah's ark and an archbishop?
28. How do we know David was older than Goliath?
29. How did Jonah feel when swallowed by the great fish?
30. Who introduced salt meat into the navy?
31. What did Adam and Eve do when driven out of Eden?
32. Why couldn't Adam and Eve gamble?

6. None—they were all born small, as all babies are.
7. Flood lights.
8. A lawyer studies the law and the profits.
9. Jonah—even a whale couldn't keep him down.
10. Samson—he brought the house down even though it was filled with his enemies (Judges 16:27-30).
11. Joseph—he was taken from the family circle and put in the pit (Genesis 37:3-24).
12. Noah—he had a boatful of preserved pairs.
13. He went 150 days and nights without finding Ararat (e'er a rat).
14. Parents.
15. Nicodemus, since he was a ruler (John 3:1).
16. Joseph was overseeing and Zacchaeus was seeing over.
17. Jesus had dinner with a sinner, and the fish had a sinner for dinner.
18. They both raised a prophet.
19. Bareskin.
20. Wet.
21. Enoch, his father, never died—he was taken into heaven.
22. Early in the fall.
23. "King Ahaz cut off the borders of the bases" (2 Kings 16:17).
24. Joseph—the pharaoh made a ruler of him.
25. He had poor comforters.
26. Eve.
27. One was a high ark, the other is a hierarch.
28. He rocked Goliath to sleep.
29. Down in the mouth.
30. Noah, who took Ham into the ark.
31. They raised Cain.
32. God took their Paradise (pair o' dice) away.

33. Who presented Adam with a walking stick?
34. Who, besides Adam and Melchizedek, had neither father nor mother?
35. Who slept five in a bed?
36. Why didn't Moses take hornets into the ark?
37. Who was the first person to have surgery performed on him?
38. How do we know Abraham was smart?
39. What is the first game mentioned in the Bible?
40. What son of Noah was a real clown?
41. Why couldn't Cain please God with his offering?
42. Why wouldn't the rooster fight on the ark?
43. How were the disciples cruel to corn?
44. What minor affliction brought about Samson's death?
45. Who was the Bible's first financial wizard?
46. What did Noah say as he was loading the ark?
47. How did Adam and Eve feel when they left the garden?
48 Who is the first king in the Bible?
49. Who is the first man in the Bible?
50. Who is the first woman in the Bible?
51. Who was the shortest man in the Bible?
52. Who was the first electrician in the Bible?
53. Who was the smallest man in the Bible?

✦All Kinds of Villains

1. Who plotted to have the entire Hebrew nation completely exterminated?
2. Who committed the first murder?
3. Who acknowledged the innocence of Jesus but allowed him to be crucified anyway?
4. Who made numerous attempts to swindle Jacob, who ultimately prospered?

33. Eve—she presented him with a little Cain.
34. Joshua, the son of Nun.
35. David, who slept with his forefathers.
36. Moses didn't go on the ark.
37. Adam—God removed one of his ribs.
38. He knew a Lot.
39. Adam and Eve played hide-and-seek with God.
40. Ham.
41. He just wasn't Abel.
42. He was chicken.
43. They pulled its ears.
44. Fallen arches.
45. Noah—he floated his stock while the whole world was in liquidation.
46. "Now I herd everything."
47. A little put out.
48. King James, if you have the King James Version—he's mentioned in the dedication.
49. Chap. 1.
50. Genesis (Jenny's sis).
51. Nehemiah (Knee-high-miah) or Bildad the Shuhite (Shoe-height).
52. Noah—he unloaded his family and the animals and made the ark light (arc light).
53. Peter, who slept on his watch (Matthew 26:40).

✦All Kinds of Villains (Answers)

1. Haman, minister of Persia (Esther).
2. Cain, who murdered his brother (Genesis 4:8).
3. Pontius Pilate (John 18–19).
4. Laban, his father-in-law (Genesis 29–31).

5. What king was constantly making oaths of love and loyalty to David while frequently trying to kill him?
6. What evil king of Israel was led into even more wickedness by his beautiful and scheming wife?
7. Who ordered the killing of infant boys in Bethlehem?
8. What treacherous son led a revolt against his father, the king of Israel?
9. What ruler, who had already had John the Baptist beheaded, was Jesus made to appear before?
10. What two traitorous army captains murdered their king as a favor to David and were then executed by David for treachery?

◆Thieving Types

1. Who stole idols from her father?
2. What robber was released from prison at the time of the Passover?
3. According to Malachi, what were the people of Judah stealing from God?
4. Who was stoned for stealing booty during the battle for Ai?
5. Which epistles say that the day of the Lord will come like a thief?
6. What disciple stole from the treasury?
7. In the time of the judges, what man stole eleven hundred pieces of silver from his own mother?
8. What did Joseph accuse his brothers of stealing?
9. What prophet condemns people who pile up stolen goods?

5. Saul (1 Samuel 19–17).
6. Ahab, husband of Jezebel (1 Kings 16).
7. Herod, known to history as Herod the Great (Matthew 2:16).
8. Absalom, son of David (2 Samuel 15).
9. Herod Antipas (Matthew 14:10).
10. Recab and Baanah, captains of Ishbosheth (2 Samuel 4).

✦Thieving Types (Answers)

1. Rachel (Genesis 31:19).
2. Barabbas (John 18:40).
3. The tithes they owed (Malachi 3:8).
4. Achan (Joshua 7:10-26).
5. 1 Thessalonians (5:2) and 2 Peter (3:10).
6. Judas Iscariot (John 12:4-6).
7. Micah (Judges 17:1-4).
8. His silver cup (Genesis 44:1-17).
9. Habakkuk (2:6).

✦Playing with Fire

1. What group of converts burned their books of magic?
2. Who burned Joab's barley field just to get his attention?
3. Who burned the Philistines' grain by tying torches to the tails of foxes?
4. What king of Babylon burned Jerusalem?
5. What Canaanite city was burned down by the men of Dan?
6. What Israelite had his goods burned after he had been stoned to death?
7. What nation burned David's city of Ziklag?
8. What king committed suicide by burning down his palace with himself inside?
9. What judge killed about a thousand people when he burned down the tower of Shechem?
10. What Israelite city was burned up by Pharaoh?
11. What tribe of Israel sacked Jerusalem and burned it?
12. In the days of the judges, what tribe had its cities burned by the other tribes?

✦People in Exile

1. What apostle was exiled to the island of Patmos?
2. How many years were the Israelites in Egypt?
3. What prophet was exiled in Egypt with other people from Judah?
4. What was the first instance of exile in the Bible?
5. Who was brought down to Egypt and sold to a man named Potiphar?
6. Who chose to go into exile rather than constantly quarrel with his brother?
7. Who was exiled from the rest of the world?
8. Who did Abraham banish to the desert?

✦Playing with Fire (Answers)

1. The Ephesians (Acts 19:19).
2. Absalom (2 Samuel 14:28-33).
3. Samson (Judges 15:4-5).
4. Nebuchadnezzar (2 Kings 25:9).
5. Laish (Judges 18:26-27).
6. Achan (Joshua 7:24-25).
7. The Amalekites (1 Samuel 30:1).
8. Zimri (1 Kings 16:18).
9. Abimelech (Judges 9:49).
10. Gezer (1 Kings 9:16).
11. Judah (Judges 1:8).
12. Benjamin (Judges 20:48).

✦People in Exile (Answers)

1. John (Revelation 1:9).
2. 430 years (Exodus 12:40).
3. Jeremiah (43:5-7).
4. God drove Adam and Eve out of the garden (Genesis 3:24).
5. Joseph (Genesis 39:1).
6. Jacob (Genesis 27:41-45).
7. Noah and his family, since everyone else died (Genesis 7:23).
8. Hagar and Ishmael (Genesis 21:14).

9. Who stayed in Egypt until Herod died?
10. Who carried the people of Jerusalem off to Babylon?
11. What future king of Israel fled from Solomon and hid in Egypt?
12. What nation carried Israel into exile?
13. Who was in exile three years after killing his brother Amnon?
14. What land did Moses flee to when he left Egypt?
15. Who was exiled to the land of Nod?
16. What judge fled from his kin and lived in the land of Tob?
17. Christians were scattered throughout Judea and Samaria because of a persecution that began after whose death?
18. What exiled king of Judah became a friend of the king of Babylon?
19. Who predicted the Babylonian exile to Hezekiah?
20. Who was king in Israel when the Assyrians deported the people?
21. What king of Judah was temporarily exiled in Assyria, where he repented of his evil ways?
22. Who was king when Jerusalem fell to the Babylonians?
23. What prophet went into exile in Babylon?
24. Who was appointed governor of Judah after the people went into exile?
25. When the Assyrians deported the people of Israel, how many of the twelve original tribes were left?
26. What blind king died in exile in Babylon?
27. What king issued an edict ending the exile of the Jews?
28. What Assyrian king carried the people of Israel into exile?
29. What interpreter of dreams was in exile in Babylon?
30. What prophet warned the wicked priest Amaziah that Israel would go into exile?

9. Joseph, Mary, and Jesus (Matthew 2:13-15).
10. Nebuchadnezzar (2 Kings 24:14-15).
11. Jeroboam (1 Kings 11:40).
12. Assyria (2 Kings 17:6).
13. Absalom (2 Samuel 13:37-38).
14. Midian (Exodus 2:15).
15. Cain (Genesis 4:13-16).
16. Jephthah (Judges 11:3).
17. Stephen's (Acts 8:1).
18. Jehoiachin (2 Kings 25:27-30).
19. Isaiah (2 Kings 20:12-19).
20. Pekah (2 Kings 15:29).
21. Manasseh (2 Chronicles 33:11-13).
22. Zedekiah (2 Chronicles 36:11-20).
23. Ezekiel (1:1-2).
24. Gedaliah (2 Kings 25:22).
25. One—Judah (2 Kings 17:18).
26. Zedekiah (Jeremiah 52:11).
28. Cyrus of Persia (2 Chronicles 36:22-23).
28. Tiglath-Pileser (2 Kings 15:29).
29. Daniel (1:1-6).
30. Amos (7:17).

31. Which epistles are addressed to God's people in exile?
32. Which psalm is a lament of the exiles in Babylon?

◆A Collection of Traitors

1. What infamous Philistine woman tricked Samson into revealing the secret of his strength?
2. What son of David led a major revolt against his father?
3. When Pekah the usurper reigned in Israel, who murdered him and took over the throne?
4. What fiery chariot driver slew the king of Israel and the king of Judah and later had Jezebel murdered, after which he reigned as king in Israel?
5. Hazael of Syria usurped the throne after he murdered the king, Ben-hadad. What unusual method did he use for the murder?
6. What traitor murdered Elah, king of Israel, and then later, after a seven-day reign, committed suicide?
7. Who murdered Shallum and took his place on the throne of Israel?
8. When Judas appeared in Gethsemane to betray Jesus, he was accompanied by a crowd. What were the people of the crowd carrying?

◆A Gallery of Prisoners

1. Who was put in prison as a political enemy of the Philistines?
2. What king of Israel was imprisoned for defying Assyrian authority?
3. What kinsman of Jesus was imprisoned for criticizing King Herod's marriage to Herodias?

31. James and 1 Peter.
32. Psalm 137.

✦A Collection of Traitors (Answers)

1. Delilah (Judges 16).
2. Absalom (2 Samuel 15).
3. Hoshea (2 Kings 15:30).
4. Jehu (2 Kings 9).
5. He took a thick cloth, dipped it in water, and smothered the king (2 Kings 8:15).
6. Zimri (1 Kings 16:8-10).
7. Menahem (2 Kings 15:14).
8. Swords and clubs (Mark 14:43).

✦A Gallery of Prisoners (Answers)

1. Samson (Judges 16:24).
2. Hoshea (2 Kings 17:4).
3. John the Baptist (Matthew 14:3-5).

4. What famous dreamer was imprisoned after being accused of trying to seduce Potiphar's wife?
5. Whose brothers were imprisoned after being falsely accused of being spies in Egypt?
6. Who was imprisoned for prophesying the destruction of the kingdom of Judah?
7. What king of Judah was blinded and imprisoned because he defied Babylonian authority?
8. Who prophesied doom for King Asa and was put in prison?
9. What king of Judah was sent into exile in Babylon and put in prison, but was later released and treated as a friend of the king of Babylon?
10. Who prophesied doom and defeat for King Ahab and was put in prison for his harsh words?
11. What two apostles were put into prison in Jerusalem for preaching the gospel?
12. Who remained in the prison at Philippi even after an earthquake opened the prison doors?

✦Courts, Councils, and Trials

1. When Jesus was brought before the Council, how many false witnesses were brought in to accuse him?
2. Who suggested to Moses that he appoint judges so that he would not have to judge all cases himself?
3. According to the Law, how many witnesses are necessary before a man could be tried and put to death?
4. What cynical king asked Jesus questions and then allowed him to be mocked?
5. According to Jesus, when his followers were dragged into court, they would not need to worry about their defense, for someone else would speak through them. Who?

4. Joseph (Genesis 39:7-19).
5. Joseph's (Genesis 42).
6. Jeremiah (37–38).
7. Zedekiah (2 Kings 25:6-7).
8. Hanani (2 Chronicles 16:10).
9. Jehoiachin (2 Kings 24:12; 25:27-30).
10. Micaiah (1 Kings 22:26-27).
11. Peter and John (Acts 4:3).
12. Paul and Silas (Acts 16:16-24).

✦Courts, Councils, and Trials (Answers)

1. Two (Matthew 26:57-66).
2. His father-in-law, Jethro (Exodus 18).
3. At least two (Deuteronomy 17:6).
4. Herod (Luke 23:1-11).
5. The Spirit (Matthew 10:16-20).

6. What stinging accusation of the Jews finally convinced Pilate to allow Jesus to be executed?

7. What person's presence at the trial of Peter and John kept the rulers and priests from punishing the two apostles?

8. When Stephen was brought to trial, what was the charge laid against him?

9. In what city were Paul and Silas tried, flogged, and jailed after they cast a demon out of a fortune-teller?

10. When Paul was mobbed in the temple, who rescued him?

11. What Roman official gave Paul a centurion as a guard and told the centurion to allow Paul freedom to see whomever he wished?

12. What three rulers, hearing Paul defend himself in Caesarea, agreed that he deserved no punishment?

✦Lies and More Lies

1. Who was the first person to lie to God about a murder?

2. Who was probably the most deceptive future father-in-law in the Bible?

3. What doting mother lied to procure a blessing for her favorite son?

4. What frustrated Egyptian wife claimed her Hebrew servant tried to seduce her?

5. What lying prophet put Jeremiah in the stocks and was later told that he and his whole household would die in exile?

6. Who was turned into a leper for lying to the prophet Elisha?

7. What owner of a vineyard was executed by Ahab because lying witnesses claimed he had blasphemed against God and the king?

6. They claimed that Pilate was no friend of Caesar (John 19:12).
7. The lame man Peter and John had healed (Acts 4:14).
8. That he had taught that Jesus had aimed to change the customs taught by Moses (Acts 6:11-14).
9. Philippi (Acts 16:16-22).
10. The chief Roman captain (Acts 22:30; 23:1-10).
11. Felix (Acts 24:23).
12. Festus, Agrippa, and Bernice (Acts 25:23—26:32).

◆Lies and More Lies (Answers)

1. Cain (Genesis 4:8-9).
2. Laban, father-in-law of Jacob (Genesis 29).
3. Rebecca, mother of Jacob and Esau (Genesis 27).
4. The wife of Potiphar, Joseph's master (Genesis 39).
5. Pashur (Jeremiah 20:1-3, 6).
6. His servant, Gehazi (2 Kings 5:20-27).
7. Naboth (1 Kings 21).

8. What king of Israel claimed to be a devout worshiper of Baal in order to gather together Baal-worshipers and butcher them?
9. Who died after lying to Peter about the value of the possessions they had sold?
10. What godly prophet lied to Ahab about the outcome of a battle?
11. What two men—father and son—claimed at different times that their wives were actually their sisters?

✦Violent People and Things

1. What oversized warrior had bronze armor weighing over 125 pounds?
2. What Roman official in Jerusalem bowed to the wishes of an uncontrollable mob?
3. In what city in Greece did a group of Jews whip up a company of thugs in an anti-Paul riot?
4. Who carried five smooth stones as his weapons?
5. What did Ehud use to kill fat King Eglon of Moab?
6. Who killed six hundred Philistines with an ox goad?
7. What did Jael use to murder Sisera?
8. What rebel was killed by three darts, shot into his heart by Joab?
9. What prophet was commanded to make a model of Jerusalem and set battering rams against it?
10. Who threw a javelin at David?
11. In what city was Jesus almost killed by an angry mob?
12. What city had a riot on behalf of the goddess Artemis?
13. What king fortified Jerusalem with catapults for throwing stones?
14. What apostle was almost done in by forty men waiting to ambush him at Jerusalem?

8. Jehu (2 Kings 10).
9. Ananias and Sapphira (Acts 5:1-9).
10. Micaiah (1 Kings 22).
11. Abraham (Genesis 12:11-13) and Isaac (26:6-7).

◆Violent People and Things (Answers)

1. Goliath (1 Samuel 17:4-6).
2. Pilate (Matthew 27:23-24).
3. Thessalonica (Acts 17:5).
4. David (1 Samuel 17:40).
5. A two-edged dagger (Judges 3:16-21).
6. Shamgar (Judges 3:31).
7. A tent peg through his temple (Judges 4:17-21).
8. Absalom (2 Samuel 18:14).
9. Ezekiel (19:34).
10. Saul (1 Samuel 18:11).
11. Nazareth (Luke 4:29).
12. Ephesus (Acts 19:28-29).
13. Uzziah (2 Chronicles 26:14-15).
14. Paul (Acts 23:21-23).

15. Who drew the army of Ai out of the city while another group ambushed the city and destroyed it?
16. What paranoid king ordered the execution of the infants in Bethlehem?
17. Who killed Abner?
18. What evil king of Judah was killed by his servants?
19. What Christian witness was killed by the people of Pergamos?
20. Who killed Ben-Hadad with a wet cloth?
21. What two women brought about the execution of John the Baptist?
22. What king of Israel had the whole dynasty of Ahab murdered?
23. What former member of the Egyptian court killed an Egyptian official?
24. Who did Rechab and Baanah murder to get in good with David?
25. What king of Assyria was murdered at worship by his two sons?
26. What good king of Judah was murdered by his court officials?
27. What saintly deacon was murdered by the Jewish elders for his testimony?
28. Who had one of his army men killed in order to cover up an adulterous affair?
29. Who killed Hamor and Shechem for offending their sister Dinah?
30. What Old Testament figure boasted to his two wives that he had killed a young man?
31. What son of Abraham was supposed to have been against everyone, and everyone against him?
32. Who caused a riot when people thought he had taken a Gentile into the temple?
33. What tribe was ambushed at Gibeah by the other tribes of Israel?
34. In the time of the judges, what did the Levite do when his concubine had been savagely abused by the men of Gibeah?

15. Joshua (8:12-22).
16. Herod (Matthew 2:16).
17. Joab (2 Samuel 3:27).
18. Amon (2 Kings 21:23).
19. Antipas (Revelation 2:13).
20. Hazael (2 Kings 8:7, 15).
21. Herodias and her daughter (Mark 6:25, 27).
22. Jehu (2 Kings 9).
23. Moses (Exodus 2:12).
24. Ishbosheth (2 Samuel 4:6).
25. Sennacherib (2 Kings 19:37).
26. Joash (2 Kings 12:20-21).
27. Stephen (Acts 7:58-59).
28. David (2 Samuel 12:9).
29. Levi and Simeon (Genesis 34:26).
30. Lamech (Genesis 34:26).
31. Ishmael (Genesis 16:12).
32. Paul (Acts 21:30-35).
33. Benjamin (Judges 20:29-33).
34. He cut her into twelve pieces and sent a piece to each tribe of Israel.

35. Who killed Amasa after holding his beard and kissing him?
36. What rebel killed Gedaliah, the governor of Judah after the fall of Judah to the Babylonians?
37. Where did Cain kill Abel?
38. What king was critically wounded by Philistine arrows?
39. Who slew a thousand men with the jawbone of an ass?
40. Who carried a staff that was as big as a weaver's beam?
41. Who pelted King David with stones while telling him what a violent king he was?

◆The Impersonators

1. What king disguised himself in order to consult with a sorceress?
2. Who fooled Jacob by posing as her sister?
3. Who pretended to be a madman in order to escape from King Achish?
4. Who disguised himself while going to battle against the forces of Pharaoh Neco of Egypt?
5. Who posed as her husband's sister while in Egypt?
6. What king's wife disguised herself in order to consult the prophet Ahijah?
7. What smooth-skinned man disguised himself so well that he passed himself off as his hairy brother?
8. Who persuaded the clever woman of Tekoa to pretend to be a widow in order to play on David's sympathy?
9. Who posed as Isaac's sister?
10. Who fooled Joshua by pretending to be ambassadors from a distant country?
11. What evil king of Israel disguised himself while going against the armies of Syria?

35. Joab (2 Samuel 20:9-10).
36. Ishmael (2 Kings 25:25).
37. Out in the fields (Genesis 4:8).
38. Saul (1 Samuel 31:3).
39. Samson (Judges 15:15).
40. Goliath (1 Samuel 17:7).
41. Shimei (2 Samuel 16:5-8).

✦The Impersonators (Answers)

1. Saul (1 Samuel 28:8).
2. Leah (Genesis 29:21-25).
3. David (1 Samuel 21:12—22:1).
4. King Josiah (2 Chronicles 35:20-24).
5. Sarai, wife of Abram (Genesis 12:10-20).
6. Jeroboam's (1 Kings 14:1-6).
7. Jacob (Genesis 27:1-29).
8. Joab (2 Samuel 14:1-24).
9. His wife Rebekah (Genesis 26:6-11).
10. The Gibeonites (Joshua 9:4-16).
11. Ahab (1 Kings 22:30-40).

12. Who sent spies to act as followers of Jesus and to try to trap him?
13. What king was confronted by a prophet posing as a wounded soldier?
14. According to Paul, who masquerades as an angel of light?

✦Naughty Ladies

1. What judge of Israel was a prostitute's son?
2. What two New Testament epistles speak of the righteousness of the prostitute Rahab?
3. What king served as judge when two prostitutes fought over a child?
4. Who had a vision of a prostitute with a city's name engraved on her head?
5. What character in a parable wasted his money on prostitutes?
6. According to Jesus, what prophet had prostitutes and tax collectors as followers?
7. What prophet did the Lord tell about two prostitutes named Oholah and Oholibah?
8. Where did the prostitute Rahab live?
9. Who ordered his daughter-in-law Tamar burned because she had acted like a prostitute?
10. Who married a faithless woman named Gomer?
11. Who went on a killing spree when their sister Dinah was treated like a prostitute?
12. Who tricked the people of Gaza by leaving a prostitute's house earlier than they expected?
13. What epistle warns Christians against patronizing prostitutes?

12. The chief priests and scribes (Luke 20:19-20).
13. Ahab (1 Kings 20:35-43).
14. Satan (2 Corinthians 11:14).

✦Naughty Ladies (Answers)

1. Gideon (Judges 11:1).
2. James (2:25) and Hebrews (11:31).
3. Solomon (1 Kings 3:16).
4. John (Revelation 17:5).
5. The prodigal son (Luke 15:30).
6. John the Baptist (Matthew 21:32).
7. Ezekiel (23:1-21).
8. Jericho (Joshua 2:1-6).
9. Judah (Genesis 38:24).
10. Hosea (chapters 1-3).
11. Levi and Simeon (Genesis 34:25-31).
12. Samson (Judges 16:1-3).
13. 1 Corinthians (6:15-16).

14. What prophet warned the priest Amaziah that his wife would become a prostitute?
15. According to tradition, what follower of Jesus had been a prostitute, though the Bible does not refer to her as one?

◆Sexual Sinning

1. Who had two daughters who got him drunk and committed incest?
2. What church in Greece had a scandalous member who was cohabiting with his stepmother?
3. How many times had the immoral Samaritan woman, who was living with her present lover, been married?
4. What son of David forced his half-sister to have sexual relations with him?
5. What book of the Old Testament mentions a gang rape of a concubine belonging to a Levite?
6. What daughter-in-law of Judah enticed him to have relations with her?
7. What Israelite sinned in the wilderness by taking a Midianite woman as his harlot companion?
8. What daughter of Jacob was raped by Shechem?
9. What city has given its name to homosexual behavior?
10. Who was killed by God because he spilled out his seed on the ground rather than fathering a child by his brother's wife?
11. What sin were the men of Gibeah hoping to commit when they stormed the house of a man who had taken in a traveler?
12. What priest had two sons who slept with the women who worked at the entrance of the tabernacle?
13. What beautiful woman committed adultery with David?

14. Amos (7:17).
15. Mary Magdalene.

✦Sexual Sinning (Answers)

 1. Lot (Genesis 19:30-38).
 2. Corinth (1 Corinthians 5:1).
 3. Five (John 4).
 4. Amnon (2 Samuel 13:14).
 5. Judges (19:22-28).
 6. Tamar (Genesis 38:14-18).
 7. Zimri (Numbers 25:6-14).
 8. Dinah (Genesis 34:1-2).
 9. Sodom.
10. Onan (Genesis 38:9).
11. Homosexual rape (Judges 19:22).
12. Eli (1 Samuel 2:22).
13. Bathsheba (2 Samuel 11).

14. What son of Jacob had sexual relations with one of his father's concubines?
15. Who had sex with his father's concubines on the palace roof while everyone was watching?
16. What prophet's wife was a harlot before marriage and an adulteress afterward?
17. What church was home to a sexually immoral woman named Jezebel?
18. What king did John the Baptist call an adulterer?
19. What sexual sin did Paul see as the result of not worshipping the true God?
20. According to the Law, what is the punishment for committing adultery?

◆Taxes, Extortion, and Bribes

1. What noble prophet's sons were notorious for taking bribes?
2. What tax collector climbed a tree to see Jesus?
3. Who kept Paul in prison, hoping Paul would try to bribe him for release?
4. Who advised that the Egyptians be taxed 20 percent of their produce in order to prepare for famine?
5. Who taxed the Israelites in order to pay off Pul, the king of Assyria?
6. Who did Jesus send fishing in order to get money for taxes?
7. Who warned the people of Israel that having a king would mean having taxation?
8. What figure did Jesus use as a contrast to the humble tax collector?
9. What did the hungry Esau give up to Jacob in exchange for food?
10. What was Judas given to betray Jesus?
11. By what other name was the tax collector Matthew known?

14. Reuben (Genesis 35:22).
15. Absalom (2 Samuel 16:22).
16. Gomer, wife of Hosea (1–2).
17. Thyatira (Revelation 2:20).
18. Herod (Mark 6:17).
19. Homosexuality (Romans 1:26-27).
20. Death (Leviticus 20:10).

✦Taxes, Extortion, and Bribes (Answers)

1. Samuel's (1 Samuel 8:1-3).
2. Zacchaeus (Luke 19:1-10).
3. Felix (Acts 24:26).
4. Joseph (Genesis 41:34).
5. King Menahem (2 Kings 15:19-20).
6. Peter (Matthew 17:24-27).
7. Samuel (1 Samuel 8).
8. A Pharisee (Luke 18:9-14).
9. His birthright (Genesis 25:29-34).
10. Thirty pieces of silver (Matthew 26: 14-16).
11. Levi (Luke 5:29-32).

12. What did John the Baptist tell the tax collectors who came to him for baptism?
13. Who offered Delilah silver if she could find out the secret of Samson's strength?
14. Who bribed the guards at Jesus' tomb to say that the disciples had stolen the body?
15. According to the Law, how much tax did all adult Israelites have to pay when the census was taken?
16. What ruler imposed tax in Jesus' day?
17. Who taxed his subjects in order to pay tribute to Pharaoh Necho of Egypt?
18. What king is remembered as placing a "heavy yoke" of taxation on Israel?
19. What king of Israel paid tribute money to King Shalmaneser of Assyria?
20. Who laid a tax on the whole Persian empire?
21. To what king of Judah did the Philistines bring tribute?
22. What Persian king exempted the priests and Levites from paying taxes?
23. What empire's taxation led to Jesus being born in Bethlehem?
24. Whose wife was threatened with having her family's house burned down unless she would find the answer to Samson's riddle?
25. Who made for Jesus a feast that was attended by many tax collectors?

✦They Spied

1. Who sent spies to watch Jesus?
2. How many spies did Moses send into Canaan?
3. Who sent spies to see if Saul had followed him?
4. What tribe sent out five spies to check out its land?
5. What counselor of Absalom was actually a spy for David?

12. To collect no more than was legal (Luke 3:12-13).
13. The lords of the Philistines (Judges 16:5).
14. The chief priests (Matthew 28:11-15).
15. A half-shekel each (Exodus 30:12-16).
16. Caesar (Matthew 22:17-22).
17. Jehoiakim (2 Kings 23:33-35).
18. Solomon (1 Kings 12:1-14).
19. Hoshea (2 Kings 17:3-4).
20. King Ahasuerus (Esther 10:1).
21. Jehoshaphat (2 Chronicles 17:11).
22. Artaxerxes (Ezra 7:24).
23. Rome (Luke 2:1-7).
24. Samson's (Judges 14:15).
25. Levi (or Matthew) (Luke 5:29-32).

◆They Spied (Answers)

1. The chief priests and scribes (Luke 20:20).
2. Twelve—one from each tribe (Numbers 13:1-16).
3. David (1 Samuel 26:3-4).
4. Dan (Judges 18:2-28).
5. Hushai (2 Samuel 15:32-37).

6. Who sent two spies to Jericho?
7. What epistle warns against people sent in to "spy out our liberty"?
8. What rebel sent his spies throughout Israel, telling them to wait till they heard the sound of the trumpet?
9. What Canaanite city did spies find the entrance of?

✦Military Men

1. Who was sleeping between two soldiers when he was miraculously delivered?
2. What captain of the palace guard did Joseph serve under?
3. What loyal Israelite soldier gave Joshua a positive report about the land of Canaan?
4. What Hittite soldier was put on the front lines of battle so David could take his wife?
5. Which Gospel is the only one to mention the Roman soldier's piercing Jesus' body with a spear?
6. What Gittite soldier supported David during the rebellion of Absalom?
7. What leper was commander of the Syrian troops?
8. What soldier led a revolt against King Elah, made himself king, and then committed suicide after a seven-day reign?
9. What Roman soldier treated Paul kindly on his voyage to Rome?
10. What foreign king had Nebuzaradan as commander of his troops?
11. Who was commander of the rebel army when Absalom rebelled against David?
12. What Roman soldier was led to Christ by Peter?
13. Which Gospel does not mention the Roman soldier on Calvary who said, "Truly this was a son of God"?
14. Where was Jesus when a Roman officer asked him to heal a beloved servant?

6. Joshua (2:1).
7. Galatians (2:4).
8. Absalom (2 Samuel 15:10).
9. Bethel (Judges 1:23-25).

✦Military Men (Answers)

1. Peter (Acts 12:6).
2. Potiphar (Genesis 39:1).
3. Caleb (Joshua 14:6-13).
4. Uriah (2 Samuel 11:3).
5. John (19:34).
6. Ittai (2 Samuel 15:19).
7. Naaman (2 Kings 5:1).
8. Zimri (1 Kings 16:9-20).
9. Julius (Acts 27:1-3).
10. Nebuchadnezzar (2 Kings 25:8).
11. Amasa (2 Samuel 17:25).
12. Cornelius (Acts 10:1).
13. John.
14. Capernaum (Luke 7:1-5).

15. Who had a nephew that informed the Roman soldiers of a plot to kill a prisoner?
16. What was the name of the military commander who sent Paul from Jerusalem to Caesarea?
17. What soldier was in charge of David's bodyguard?
18. Where was Paul when a Roman soldier stopped him from being murdered by an angry mob?
19. What cousin of Saul was commander of the king's troops?
20. What Canaanite commander was murdered by Jael?
21. Who was commander of the Israelites under Moses?
22. Who was the commander of Abimelech's army?
23. Who met the commander of the Lord's army?
24. What judge from Gilead was called to be a commander against the Ammonites?
25. What irate soldier falsely accused Jeremiah of deserting to the Babylonians and arrested him?
26. What Philistine soldier was slain by a boy carrying a bag of stones?
27. Who was commander of Solomon's army?
28. Who was commander of David's army?
29. What commander led a successful revolt against the ill-fated King Zimri?
30. What army commander was anointed by a prophet and told that he was to stamp out Ahab's dynasty?
31. What Assyrian field commander tried to intimidate King Hezekiah by speaking propaganda to the people of Jerusalem?
32. Who was commander of the troops during the rebuilding of the walls of Jerusalem?
33. What Babylonian soldier was ordered to execute Daniel and his friends?
34. What soldier, David's oldest brother, picked at David for coming to the battle lines?
35. What brother of Joab was famous for having killed 300 enemy soldiers in battle?
36. Who told Roman soldiers to be content with their pay and to avoid taking money by force?

15. Paul (Acts 23:16-22).
16. Claudius Lysias (Acts 23:26).
17. Benaiah (2 Samuel 8:18).
18. Outside the temple (Acts 21:30-33).
19. Abner (1 Samuel 14:50).
20. Sisera (Judges 4:2).
21. Joshua (Exodus 17:10).
22. Phicol (Genesis 21:22).
23. Joshua (5:14).
24. Jephthah (Judges 11:6).
25. Irijah (Jeremiah 37:13).
26. Goliath (1 Samuel 17:48-54).
27. Benaiah (1 Kings 4:4).
28. Joab (2 Samuel 8:16).
29. Omri (1 Kings 16:16).
30. Jehu (2 Kings 9:1-11).
31. Rabshakeh (2 Kings 18:17-37).
32. Hananiah (Nehemiah 7:2).
33. Arioch (Daniel 2:14).
34. Eliab (1 Samuel 17:28).
35. Abishai (1 Chronicles 11:20).
36. John the Baptist (Luke 3:14).

✦A Bevy of Priests

1. What priest in the Bible is mentioned as having no mother or father?
2. What Hebrew married the daughter of an Egyptian priest?
3. What was the penalty in Israel for disobeying a priest?
4. What priest was made mute because he did not believe the prophecy given by an angel?
5. What oil was supposed to be used to anoint Israel's priests?
6. What priest made the first piggy bank by placing a chest with a hole in it near the altar of the temple?
7. What righteous king fired all the priests that had been appointed to serve pagan gods?
8. What are the only books of the Bible named after priests?
9. What kind of head covering did the priest wear?
10. What book mentions the priest of Israel more than any other?
11. What priests—two of Aaron's sons—were killed because they offered "strange fire" to the Lord?
12. What priest was the first head of the Levites?
13. What priest was the "king of peace"?
14. What priest of Midian taught Moses how to administer justice among the Hebrews?
15. What priest in the Old Testament was also a king?
16. Who was priest during Joshua's conquest of Canaan?
17. What priest had the boy Jehoash proclaimed king, causing the death of wicked Queen Athaliah?
18. What priest scolded a distressed woman because he thought she had been drinking at the tabernacle?
19. What was engraved on the twelve stones in the high priest's breastplate?
20. What two gluttonous priests were notorious for keeping the sacrificial meat for themselves?

✦A Bevy of Priests (Answers)

1. Melchizedek (Hebrews 7:3).
2. Joseph (Genesis 41:45).
3. Death (Deuteronomy 17:12).
4. Zacharias (Luke 1:20).
5. Olive oil (Exodus 30:24).
6. Jehoiada (2 Kings 12:9).
7. Josiah (2 Kings 23:5).
8. Ezra and Ezekiel.
9. A turban (Exodus 28:39).
10. Leviticus.
11. Nadab and Abihu (Numbers 3:4).
12. Eleazar, Aaron's son (Numbers 3:32).
13. Melchizedek (Hebrews 7:2).
14. Jethro, also called Reuel (Exodus 18:13-27).
15. Melchizedek (Genesis 14:18).
16. Eleazar (Joshua 17:4).
17. Jehoiada (2 Kings 11:9-16).
18. Eli, who scolded Hannah, future mother of Samuel (1 Samuel 1:9).
19. The names of the tribes of Israel (Exodus 28:21).
20. Hophni and Phinehas (1 Samuel 2:17).

21. What reform priest was killed by the orders of King Joash, a pupil of his father?

22. What priest had a son named Ichabod, a name meaning "the glory has departed"?

23. What five men were called to be the first priests of Israel?

24. What king ordered the execution of Ahimelech and other priests because they had conspired with David?

25. Who was the only priest to escape when Saul slaughtered the eighty-five priests of Nob?

26. What priest found the Book of the Law in the temple during Josiah's reign?

27. When Adonijah tried to grab the throne of Israel, what priest took his side?

28. What high priest had John and Peter arrested after the two disciples had healed a lame man?

29. What priest was told by Jeremiah that he would be taken to Babylon as a prisoner?

30. What king of Israel sinned by appointing priests that had not been chosen by God?

31. In the time of the judges, what man was brassy enough to set up one of his sons as priest, though he had no authority to do so?

32. What priest led a reform movement in Judah, so that the people tore down their Baal temple and idols?

33. What priest of Baal was killed in Jerusalem when a reform movement threw out all the idols?

34. What were the names of the two stones worn in the high priest's breastplate and used to determine God's will?

35. What king ordered the priest Uriah to make a copy of a pagan altar he had seen in Damascus?

36. What two men were high priests during David's reign?

37. What priest received the boy Samuel as a servant?

38. When Jerusalem fell to the Babylonians, what priest was taken prisoner to Babylon?

21. Zechariah (2 Chronicles 24:21).
22. Phinehas (1 Samuel 4:21).
23. Aaron and his sons Nadab, Abihu, Eleazar, and Ithamar (Exodus 28:1).
24. Saul (1 Samuel 22:18).
25. Abiathar (1 Samuel 22:20).
26. Hilkiah (2 Kings 22:8).
27. Abiathar (1 Kings 1:7).
28. Annas (Acts 4:6).
29. Passhur (Jeremiah 20:6).
30. Jeroboam (1 Kings 13:33).
31. Micah (Judges 17:5).
32. Jehoiada (2 Kings 11:17-20).
33. Mattan (2 Kings 11:18).
34. Urim and Thummim (Exodus 28:30).
35. Ahaz (2 Kings 16:11).
36. Abiathar and Zadok (2 Samuel 20:26).
37. Eli (1 Samuel 2:11).
38. Seraiah (2 Kings 25:18).

39. What king reversed the reform policies of Jehoiada the priest immediately after Jehoiada died?

40. What fat priest of Israel died when he heard the ark had been captured?

41. What priest scolded King Uzziah for daring to offer incense to God?

42. What leader after the exile traced his ancestry back to the high priest Aaron?

43. What kinds of objects were around the hem of the priest's robe?

44. During Nehemiah's ministry, what priest dedicated the newly rebuilt walls of Jerusalem?

45. Who is the first priest mentioned in the Bible?

46. What book of the Bible mentions a "priest forever, after the order of Melchizedek"?

47. What priest served as a witness when Isaiah gave his son the bizarre name Maher-shalal-hash-baz?

48. What evil priest had Jeremiah beaten and placed in chains?

49. What priest was banished by Solomon, fulfilling a prophecy that Eli's descendants would be stripped of the priesthood?

50. What priest received a letter criticizing him for not putting an iron collar on Jeremiah's neck?

51. What priest, a prisoner in Babylon, was also a prophet?

52. What is the only parable of Jesus to have a priest as a character?

53. What prophet locked horns with the wicked priest Amaziah at Bethel?

54. What miracle of Jesus led the priests to conspire to have him executed?

55. What prophet was sent to encourage the rebuilding of the temple under the priest Joshua?

56. Who had a vision of the high priest Joshua standing beside Satan?

57. What was the affliction of the man who was healed by Jesus, then sent to the priest?

39. Joash (2 Chronicles 24:17).
40. Eli (1 Samuel 4:18).
41. Azariah (2 Chronicles 26:18).
42. Ezra (7:5).
43. Bells and pomegranates (Exodus 28:33-34).
44. Eliashib (Nehemiah 3:1).
45. Melchizedek (Genesis 14:18).
46. Psalms (110:4) or Hebrews (7:17).
47. Uriah (Isaiah 8:2).
48. Passhur (Jeremiah 20:1).
49. Abiathar (1 Kings 2:27).
50. Zephaniah (Jeremiah 29:26).
51. Ezekiel.
52. The good Samaritan (Luke 10:31).
53. Amos (7:10-17).
54. The raising of Lazarus (John 11:47).
55. Haggai.
56. Zechariah (3:1).
57. Leprosy (Matthew 8:4).

58. In what priest's home did the enemies of Jesus meet to plot against him?

59. What disciple angrily cut off the ear of the high priest's servant when Jesus was arrested?

60. What New Testament book says that God has made his people to be a kingdom of priests?

61. What crime did the high priest charge Jesus with?

62. What priest was the father of John the Baptist?

63. What priest gave David the ritual bread when David fled from Saul?

64. According to Ezekiel, what was the one kind of woman a priest could not marry?

65. What priest announced that Jesus should die because it was appropriate for one man to die for the people?

66. What priest was told by the prophet Amos that his wife would become a prostitute?

67. According to John's Gospel, what priest was the first to examine the arrested Jesus?

68. What priest anointed Solomon as king?

69. What man asked the high priest for letters of commendation so he could work in the synagogues of Damascus?

70. What two apostles were met by a priest of Zeus who tried to offer sacrifices to them?

71. What priest had seven sons who were casting out demons in the name of Jesus?

72. What high priest ordered his men to slap Paul, which caused Paul to call him a "whitewashed wall"?

73. According to the Epistle to the Hebrews, who is the present high priest of Israel?

74. According to the Epistle to the Hebrews, what Old Testament priest is Jesus like?

75. What kinsman of Moses was a priest of Midian?

76. What priest was responsible for taking the first census of Israel?

77. What New Testament epistle mentions the priesthood more than any other?

78. What tribe of Israel did all the priests spring from?

58. Caiaphas' (Matthew 26:3).
59. Peter (Matthew 26:51).
60. Revelation (1:6).
61. Blasphemy (Matthew 26:65).
62. Zechariah (Luke 1:5).
63. Ahimelech (1 Samuel 21:1-6).
64. A divorcée (Ezekiel 44:22).
65. Caiaphas (John 11:49).
66. Amaziah (Amos 7:17).
67. Annas (John 18:13).
68. Zadok (1 Kings 1:45).
69. Paul (Acts 9:2).
70. Paul and Barnabas (Acts 14:13).
71. Sceva (Acts 19:14).
72. Ananias (Acts 23:3).
73. Jesus (Hebrews 3:1).
74. Melchizedek (Hebrews 5:6).
75. Jethro, also called Reuel (Exodus 3:1).
76. Eleazar (Numbers 26:1-2).
77. Hebrews.
78. Levi.

79. What New Testament epistle tells Christians that they are all priests?
80. What priest examined Jesus before the Council?

✦The Company of Apostles

1. Who was the first apostle to be martyred?
2. Who succeeded Judas Iscariot as an apostle?
3. What apostle was a tax collector from Capernaum?
4. According to tradition, which apostle was a missionary to India?
5. What apostle was probably crucified in Rome, head downward?
6. Who was the only one of the twelve apostles not from Galilee?
7. According to tradition, how did Simon the Zealot die?
8. Who was called the beloved disciple?
9. Who, according to tradition, preached in Assyria and Persia and died a martyr in Persia?
10. Who was not one of the original twelve, though he probably labored harder for the gospel than anyone else?
11. Which apostle was traditionally supposed to have been crucified in Egypt?
12. Which apostle, originally a disciple of John the Baptist, was supposed to have been crucified on an X-shaped cross?
13. Which of the apostles were fishermen?
14. Of all the apostles, which is the only one who is supposed to have died a natural death?
15. Who is supposed to have provided the background information for the Gospel of Mark?
16. Who, according to tradition, preached in Phrygia?
17. What hard-working companion of Paul was called an apostle?

79. 1 Peter (2:9).
80. Caiaphas (Matthew 26:62).

✦The Company of Apostles (Answers)

1. James (Acts 12:1-2).
2. Matthias (Acts 1:23-26).
3. Matthew.
4. Thomas.
5. Peter.
6. Judas Iscariot.
7. Crucifixion or being sawn in pieces.
8. John.
9. Jude.
10. Paul.
11. James the Lesser.
12. Andrew.
13. Peter, Andrew, James, John.
14. John.
15. Peter.
16. Philip.
17. Barnabas (Acts 13:1-3; 14:4).

18. Who, in Romans 16, did Paul refer to as apostles?
19. Who is supposed to have been a missionary to Armenia?
20. Who preached at Pentecost?
21. Who is supposed to have suffered martyrdom in Ethiopia?
22. Who was banished to the island of Patmos?
23. Who is supposed to have been flayed to death?
24. Who is thought to have been pushed from the summit of the temple, then beaten to death?
25. By what other name was Matthew known?
26. Who is supposed to have been executed by being sawn in pieces?
27. Who doubted the resurrected Jesus?
28. What was Peter's original name?
29. Who were the sons of Zebedee?
30. Who was the apostle to the Gentiles?
31. What was Paul's original name?
32. Who brought Peter to Jesus?
33. Who had Jesus as a guest at a meal with many tax collectors?
34. Who, according to Catholic tradition, was the first pope?
35. Who requested special places for themselves in Jesus' kingdom?
36. Who is identified with Nathanael of Cana, mentioned in John 1:45?
37. Who brought Nathanael to Jesus?
38. Who said to Jesus, "My Lord and my God"?
39. Who asked Jesus to show the disciples the Father?
40. Who were the "sons of thunder"?
41. Who was with Jesus at the Transfiguration?
42. Who was the only apostle we know for sure was married?
43. In which gospel is John not mentioned by name?
44. Who spoke for all the apostles at Caesarea Philippi?
45. Who, in John's gospel, is the "son of perdition"?
46. Who criticized the woman who anointed Jesus?

18. Andronicus and Junias.
19. Bartholomew.
20. Peter (Acts 2).
21. Matthias.
22. John.
23. Bartholomew.
24. James the Lesser.
25. Levi.
26. Simon the Zealot.
27. Thomas (John 21:25).
28. Simon.
29. James and John.
30. Paul.
31. Saul.
32. Andrew.
33. Matthew (Luke 5:29).
34. Peter.
35. James and John (Mark 10:39).
36. Bartholomew.
37. Philip (John 1:43-46).
38. Thomas (John 20:28).
39. Philip (John 14:8).
40. James and John (Mark 3:17).
41. Peter, James, and John (Mark 9:2).
42. Peter (Mark 1:30).
43. John.
44. Peter (Mark 8:27-33).
45. Judas Iscariot (John 17:12).
46. Judas Iscariot (John 12:3-5).

47. Who was absent when the risen Jesus appeared to the apostles?
48. Who brought Greeks to Jesus?
49. Who had Silas as a traveling companion on his second journey?
50. Which apostles were present at the raising of Jairus's daughter?
51. Who was a Roman citizen?
52. Who healed the crippled man at the Beautiful Gate?
53. Who healed a paralytic named Aeneas in Lydda?
54. Who was baptized by a man named Ananias?
55. What was Barnabas's original name?
56. Who did the Sanhedrin put in jail for disturbing the peace?
57. Who raised a young man named Eutychus from the dead?
58. Whom did Paul oppose when he met him in Antioch?
59. Who asked Jesus why he intended to show himself to the disciples but not to the world?
60. To whom did Jesus say, "Feed my lambs"?
61. Who preached to the intellectuals of Athens?
62. Who had a vision of a sheet filled with unclean animals?
63. Who did Jesus say he would make into fishers of men?
64. Who told Jesus he had seen a man driving out demons in Jesus' name?
65. Who did Jesus take with him to Gethsemane?
66. Who expressed dismay over how to feed the five thousand?
67. Who had a beef against a Greek silversmith named Demetrius?
68. Who brought to Jesus the boy with loaves and fishes?
69. Who was reluctant to have Jesus wash his feet?
70. Who was bitten by a viper on the island of Malta?
71. What brother of Jesus does Paul call an apostle?

47. Thomas (John 20:24).
48. Philip and Andrew (John 12:20-28).
49. Paul (Acts 15-18).
50. Peter, John, and James (Mark 5:37).
51. Paul (Acts 23:27).
52. Peter and John (Acts 3:1-10).
53. Peter (Acts 9:32-35).
54. Paul (Acts 9:10-18).
55. Joseph (Acts 4:36).
56. Peter and John (Acts 4:1-4).
57. Paul (Acts 20:7-12).
58. Peter (Galatians 2:11-21).
59. Jude (John 14:22).
60. Peter (John 21:15-19).
61. Paul (Acts 17:16-34).
62. Peter (Acts 10:9-16).
63. Peter and Andrew (Mark 1:17).
64. John (Mark 9:38).
65. Peter, James, and John (Mark 14:33).
66. Philip (John 6:7).
67. Paul (Acts 19:23-41).
68. Andrew (John 6:8-9).
69. Peter (John 13:6-9).
70. Paul (Acts 28:1-6).
71. James (Galatians 1:19).

72. What young friend of Paul, a co-author of 1 Thessalonians, was an apostle?
73. What apostle, a traveling companion of Paul, was sometimes called Silvanus?
74. According to tradition, what apostle lived to a ripe old age after miraculously living through being boiled in oil?

◆Sorcerers, Witches, and So Forth

1. What emperor had a bevy of magicians and psychics who could not interpret his strange dreams?
2. What prophet called the city of Nineveh the mistress of witchcraft?
3. In what city did Paul find many believers who had formerly dabbled in witchcraft?
4. What queen of Israel practiced witchcraft?
5. What prophet claimed that Edom, Moab, Ammon, and Tyre all had sorcerers?
6. Who called on magicians to duplicate the miracles of Moses?
7. Who was the sorcerer Paul encountered on the isle of Paphos?
8. What medium was consulted by a king who had outlawed all mediums?
9. Who amazed the people of Samaria with his conjuring tricks?
10. What book states, "Thou shalt not suffer a witch to live"?
11. What book claims that witchcraft is an "abomination unto the Lord"?
12. Who told Saul that rebellion was as bad as witchcraft?

72. Timothy (1 Thessalonians 1:1; 2:7).
73. Silas (1 Thessalonians 1:1; 2:7).
74. John.

◆Sorcerers, Witches, and So Forth (Answers)

1. Nebuchadnezzar (Daniel 2:10).
2. Nahum (3:4).
3. Ephesus (Acts 19:19).
4. Jezebel (2 Kings 9:22).
5. Jeremiah (27:3-10).
6. Pharaoh (Exodus 7:11-12).
7. Elymas (Acts 13:6-8).
8. The witch of Endor, who was visited by Saul (1 Samuel 28:7-25).
9. Simon the sorcerer (Acts 8:9).
10. Exodus (22:18).
11. Deuteronomy (18:9-12).
12. Samuel (1 Samuel 15:23).

13. What epistle mentions witchcraft as one of the works of the flesh?
14. Who called on magicians to interpret his dreams about cattle?
15. What names does the New Testament give to the magicians in Pharaoh's court in the time of Moses?

◆Cave Men, Cave Women

1. Who lived in a cave with his daughters after Sodom and Gomorrah were destroyed?
2. Who trapped five Canaanite kings in the cave where they were hiding?
3. What friend of Jesus was buried in a cave?
4. What prophet, fleeing from Jezebel, hid in a cave?
5. In the time of the judges, what tribe did the Israelites hide from in caves?
6. What hero hid in caves to avoid the wrath of Saul?
7. Who hid a hundred prophets in a cave when Jezebel was trying to kill them?
8. In Saul's time, what marauding people drove the Israelites into caves?
9. Who was buried in the cave of Machpelah?
10. Who hid in a cave while God passed by?

◆Builders of Cities

1. Who built ancient Babylon?
2. Who built a city called Enoch east of Eden?
3. Who built the Egyptian treasure cities of Pithom and Raamses?
4. Who rebuilt Gezer, which had been given as a wedding gift to his Egyptian wife by her father?
5. Who built Nineveh?
6. What king of Israel built Penuel?

13. Galatians (5:20).
14. Pharaoh (Genesis 41:8).
15. Jannes and Jambres (2 Timothy 3:8).

✦Cave Men, Cave Women (Answers)

1. Lot (Genesis 19:30).
2. Joshua (10:16-27).
3. Lazarus (John 11:38).
4. Elijah (1 Kings 19:9).
5. The Midianites (Judges 6:2).
6. David (1 Samuel 22:1-2; 23:14, 29).
7. Obadiah (1 Kings 18:4).
8. The Philistines (1 Samuel 13:5-7).
9. Sarah, Abraham, Isaac, Rebekah, Leah, and Jacob (Genesis 23:19; 25:9; 35:29; 49:30-31).
10. Moses (Exodus 33:21-23).

✦Builders of Cities (Answers)

1. Nimrod (Genesis 10:8-10).
2. Cain (Genesis 4:17).
3. The enslaved Israelites (Exodus 1:11).
4. Solomon (1 Kings 9:1-17).
5. Nimrod (Genesis 10:11).
6. Jeroboam (1 Kings 12:25).

7. Who rebuilt Ramah in order to keep people from entering or leaving Judah?
8. What king of Judah built up the defenses of Bethlehem?
9. What king of Israel built the nation's capital at Samaria?
10. What man of Bethlehem rebuilt Jericho during Ahab's reign?
11. Who rebuilt Elath and restored it to Judah?
12. Who rebuilt Babylon on a grand scale?

◆Makers of Music

1. What stringed instruments did John hear in his vision of the heavenly throne?
2. Who is mentioned as the father of those who play the harp and organ?
3. What prophetess played a timbrel and led the women of Israel in a victory song after the Red Sea incident?
4. What caused Saul's "evil spirit" to leave him?
5. Who wrote over a thousand songs?
6. What is the only book of the Bible that contains numerous directions for musical accompaniment?
7. At the dedication of Solomon's temple, 120 priests played what instruments?
8. What king of Israel had 4,000 musicians who praised the Lord with instruments the king had made?
9. What prophet prophesied while accompanied by a minstrel?
10. When the foundation for the second temple was laid, the priests played trumpets. What did the Levites play?
11. What king, who was also a poet and musician, embarrassed his wife by dancing in the streets?
12. What prophetic book of the Old Testament contains musical directions?

7. Baasha, king of Israel (1 Kings 15:17).
8. Rehoboam (2 Chronicles 11:6).
9. Omri (1 Kings 16:23-24).
10. Hiel (1 Kings 16:34).
11. Azariah (2 Kings 14:22).
12. Nebuchadnezzar (Daniel 4:30).

✦Makers of Music (Answers)

1. Harps (Revelation 14:2-3).
2. Jubal (Genesis 4:21).
3. Miriam (Exodus 15:20-21).
4. David's harp playing (1 Samuel 16:23).
5. Solomon (1 Kings 4:32).
6. Psalms.
7. Trumpets (2 Chronicles 5:11-14).
8. David (1 Chronicles 23:5).
9. Elisha (2 Kings 3:15-16).
10. Cymbals (Nehemiah 12:35-36).
11. David (2 Samuel 6:16, 20).
12. Habakkuk (3:1, 3, 9, 13, 19).

✦Artsy, Craftsy Types

1. What notorious opponent of Paul was a silversmith in Ephesus?
2. What leader fashioned a brass snake?
3. Who was the first metal craftsman in the Bible?
4. What Israelite, a worker in gold, silver, brass, stone, and wood, had responsibility for furnishing the tabernacle?
5. Who built a huge ship of gopherwood?
6. What coppersmith had, according to Paul, done him great harm?
7. Who fashioned a golden calf?
8. What was the trade of Paul, Aquila, and Priscilla?
9. What craftsman from Tyre was put in charge of all the temple's bronze work?
10. What son of a goldsmith was involved in rebuilding the walls of Jerusalem?
11. What engraver and embroiderer helped construct materials for the tabernacle?

✦Looking Good, Smelling Good

1. Who had a harem with women that were "purified" with perfumes?
2. What evil queen "painted her face" before meeting with the rebel king Jehu?
3. What book mentions a woman using such perfumes as spikenard, saffron, calamus, cinnamon, frankincense, myrrh, aloes, and many others?
4. What prophet refused to use anointing oils during three weeks of mourning?
5. Who anointed Jesus' head with an expensive ointment known as spikenard?

✦Artsy, Craftsy Types (Answers)

1. Demetrius (Acts 19:24).
2. Moses (Numbers 21:9).
3. Tubal-cain (Genesis 4:22).
4. Bezaleel (Exodus 31:1-6).
5. Noah (Genesis 6:13-22).
6. Alexander (2 Timothy 4:14).
7. Aaron (Exodus 32:4).
8. Tentmaking (Acts 18:1-3).
9. Huram (1 Kings 7:13-14).
10. Uzziel (Nehemiah 3:8).
11. Aholiab (Exodus 38:23).

✦Looking Good, Smelling Good (Answers)

1. King Ahasuerus (Esther 2:12).
2. Jezebel (2 Kings 9:30).
3. The Song of Solomon.
4. Daniel (10:3).
5. Mary, Lazarus's sister (John 12:3).

6. What sweet-smelling substances were brought to the infant Jesus?
7. What Hebrew officials were anointed with holy oil perfumed with aromatic spices?
8. According to Proverbs 27:9, what do ointment and perfume do?
9. What two prophets speak critically of women putting on eye makeup?
10. What woman, portrayed in Proverbs 7, perfumed her bed with myrrh, aloes, and cinnamon?
11. Where was Jesus when a sinful woman poured an alabaster jar of perfume on his feet?
12. What man uses myrrh, frankincense, and other spices as perfumes?

◆Rings on Their Fingers

1. What dreaming ruler gave Joseph his own ring?
2. In which of Jesus' parables does a ring play a part?
3. Who did King Ahasuerus of Persia give his ring to?
4. When Daniel was sealed up in the lions' den, who placed his signet ring on the stone?
5. For what did the Israelites give up their rings and other jewelry?
6. After the death of Haman, who received the Persian king's signet ring?

◆Glad Rags

1. Who wore a camel's hair tunic?
2. What king of Israel is mentioned as wearing a crown and a gold bracelet?
3. What Egyptian official was given fine linen, the pharaoh's ring, and a gold chain for his neck?

6. Frankincense and myrrh (Matthew 2:11).
7. Israel's priests (Exodus 30:23-33).
8. "Rejoice the heart."
9. Jeremiah (4:30) and Ezekiel (23:40).
10. The adulteress.
11. At the home of Simon the Pharisee (Luke 7:36-50).
12. The male lover in the Song of Solomon.

✦Rings on Their Fingers (Answers)

1. The Pharaoh (Genesis 41:42).
2. The parable of the prodigal son (since the son was given a ring by his father upon returning home) (Luke 15:22).
3. Haman (Esther 3:10-13).
4. The king (Daniel 6:17).
5. As a freewill offering for the tabernacle (Exodus 35:22).
6. Mordecai (Esther 8:2-13).

✦Glad Rags (Answers)

1. John the Baptist (Matthew 3:4).
2. Saul (2 Samuel 1:10).
3. Joseph (Genesis 42:42).

4. What people had such well-made clothes that years of wilderness wandering did not even wear out their shoes?

5. Whose eye-catching cloak caused murderous envy in his brothers?

6. The best-dressed man in Israel wore fine colored linen with embroidered bells and pomegranates, a linen breastplate with gold and precious stones, and a gold-studded hat. Who was he?

7. What down-and-out man is mentioned as having worn a gold earring in his better days?

8. Only one person is mentioned in the Bible as having worn gloves. Who?

9. What warriors were so extravagant that even their camels wore necklaces?

10. What people wore fine Egyptian linen and purple robes?

11. What people put gold chains around their camels' necks?

✦Menservants, Maidservants

1. What runaway servant was the main subject of one of Paul's epistles?

2. Who sent two of his servants to fetch Peter from Joppa?

3. To whose servant did Peter deny any knowledge of Jesus?

4. Who, with 318 of his servants, defeated the captors of Sodom and Gomorrah?

5. Who was Elisha's servant?

6. What Egyptian official had Joseph as a servant?

7. Who was permanently crippled because a servant woman dropped him as a baby?

8. Who cut off the ear of Malchus, the high priest's servant?

4. The Israelites (Deuteronomy 29:5).
5. Joseph's (Genesis 37:3)
6. The high priest (Exodus 28).
7. Job (42:11).
8. Jacob (Genesis 27:16).
9. The Midianites (Judges 8:24-26).
10. The "princes of the sea" (Phoenicians) (Ezekiel 26:16).
11. The Midianites (Judges 8:26).

✦Menservants, Maidservants (Answers)

1. Onesimus (Philemon).
2. Cornelius (Acts 10:7-8).
3. The high priest's (John 18:26).
4. Abraham (Genesis 14:14-15).
5. Gehazi (2 Kings 4:12).
6. Potiphar (Genesis 39).
7. Mephibosheth (2 Samuel 4:4).
8. Peter (John 18:10).

9. Who had a servant girl who advised him to go to Elisha to be cured of leprosy?
10. What servant woman was the mother of Ishmael?
11. Who did Abraham's eldest servant find a wife for?
12. Where did Jesus heal a centurion's servant?
13. Who was a servant to the Persian king Artaxerxes?
14. What two servants of Pharaoh were in prison with Joseph?
15. Who was Laban's servant for many years?
16. Whose servant woman took Moses from the river?
17. What judge's servant killed him at his own request?
18. What two servant women bore children to Jacob?
19. Who made the Israelites into slaves?
20. In what parable are the servants of a landowner beaten up?
21. In what parable are servants given money to invest?
22. At whose house did Peter deny Christ to a servant girl?
23. Who was Elijah's personal servant?
24. What people were, in the time of Joshua, cursed to be Israel's servants?
25. Who was Moses' personal servant?
26. Who was Jesus responding to when he told the parable of the unmerciful servant?

◆Seven Suicides

1. What judge of Israel had his armor-bearer kill him so he would avoid the disgrace of being killed by a woman?
2. According to Matthew's account, Judas committed suicide by hanging himself. How, according to Acts, did Judas die?
3. What king of Israel, who reigned only seven days, killed himself by burning down the palace with himself inside?

9. Naaman the Syrian (2 Kings 5:2-3).
10. Hagar (Genesis 16:1).
11. Isaac (Genesis 24).
12. Capernaum (Matthew 8:13).
13. Nehemiah (1:11).
14. The chief butler and chief baker (Genesis 41).
15. Jacob (Genesis 29-31).
16. Pharaoh's daughter's (Exodus 2:5).
17. Abimelech's (Judges 9:54).
18. Bilhah and Zilpah (Genesis 30).
19. The Egyptians (Exodus 1:13).
20. The parable of the tenants (Mark 12:1-5).
21. The parable of the talents (Matthew 25:14-30).
22. The high priest's (John 18:17).
23. Elisha (2 Kings 3:11).
24. The Hivites (Joshua 9:23).
25. Joshua (Exodus 33:11).
26. Peter (Matthew 18:21-35).

✦Seven Suicides (Answers)

1. Abimelech, who had a millstone dropped on his head by a woman of Thebez (Judges 9:54).
2. He fell headlong in a field and burst open (Acts 1:18).
3. Zimri (1 Kings 16:18).

4. What king killed himself by falling on his own sword?
5. What strong man killed himself along with a houseful of Philistines?
6. What friend of Absalom was so disgraced when Absalom did not follow his advice that he went and hanged himself?
7. Who refused to obey the king's request to kill him, then followed the king in committing suicide?

◆Some Lepers

1. What leper of Bethany entertained Jesus in his home?
2. What king of Judah was a leper until the day of his death?
3. What captain of the armies of Syria was a leper?
4. What prophetess became a snow-white leper for a short time?
5. Who put his hand into his bosom and, drawing it out, found it leprous?
6. Who became a leper after he lied to the prophet Elisha?
8. What is the greatest number of lepers Jesus healed at any one time?

◆Bodies Not Fully Functional

1. Who healed the crippled man at the Beautiful Gate in Jerusalem?
2. Where was Jesus when a handicapped man's friends lowered him through the roof?
3. What grandson of Saul was crippled in both feet?

4. Saul (1 Samuel 31:5).
5. Samson (Judges 16:30).
6. Ahitophel (2 Samuel 17:23).
7. Saul's armorbearer (1 Samuel 31:5).

✦Some Lepers (Answers)

1. Simon (Mark 14:3).
2. Uzziah (2 Chronicles 26:21).
3. Naaman (2 Kings 5:1).
4. Miriam (Numbers 12:10).
5. Moses (Exodus 4:6).
6. Gehazi (2 Kings 5:27).
7. The Lord (Numbers 5:1-4).
8. Ten (Luke 17:12).

✦Bodies Not Fully Functional (Answers)

1. Peter and John (Acts 3:2).
2. Capernaum (Mark 2:5-12).
3. Mephibosheth (2 Samuel 4:4).

4. Which gospel mentions the healing of the man by the pool at Bethesda?
5. Whose servant did Jesus heal without even being physically near the man?
6. Who did Jesus heal in a synagogue on the sabbath?
7. Who healed the paralytic Aeneas?
8. What apostle healed the man in Lystra who had been crippled since birth?
9. What was the affliction of the man Jesus healed in a Galilean synagogue?
10. Who had so much faith in Jesus' healing power that she touched the hem of his robe?
11. What blind man of Jericho did Jesus heal?
12. What was the affliction of the man at the pool of Siloam?
13. When Jesus healed the blind man of Bethsaida, what did the man say was the first thing he saw?
14. What person, suffering from deafness, was healed by Jesus after the disciples failed to heal?
15. What healing led to Jesus being accused of demon possession?
16. What patriarch became so blind he couldn't tell his sons apart?
17. What sinful city entertained visitors that struck the men with blindness?
18. What priest, ninety-eight years old, was blind?
19. What army did Elisha strike with blindness?
20. What sorcerer, an opponent of Paul, was struck blind?
21. Who was blind for three days after seeing a great light?
22. What judge was blinded by the Philistines?
23. Who had King Zedekiah of Judah blinded?
24. What father of twelve sons was blind in his old age?
25. What did Jesus put in the eyes of the blind man at the pool of Siloam?
26. What blind prophet received the wife of King Jeroboam?

4. John (5:8).
 5. The centurion's (Matthew 8:13).
 6. A crippled woman (Luke 13:10-13).
 7. Peter (Acts 9:33).
 8. Paul (Acts 14:8).
 9. He had a withered hand (Matthew 12:13).
10. The woman with the issue of blood (Matthew 9:22).
11. Bartimaeus (Matthew 20:34).
12. Blind from birth (John 9:7).
13. Men, who looked like trees walking (Mark 8:25).
14. The boy near Mount Hermon (Mark 9:25).
15. The healing of a mute man in Galilee (Luke 11:14).
16. Isaac (Genesis 27:1).
17. Sodom (Genesis 19:11).
18. Eli (1 Samuel 4:15).
19. The Syrians (2 Kings 6:18).
20. Elymas (Acts 13:7-12).
21. Paul (Acts 9:9).
22. Samson (Judges 16:21).
23. Nebuchadnezzar (Jeremiah 39:7).
24. Jacob (Genesis 48:10).
25. Mud (John 9:1-7).
26. Ahijah (1 Kings 14:4).

27. What book says that blind animals must not be sacrificed to God?

28. What righteous man claimed that he acted as eyes to the blind?

✦Not to Be Taken Seriously (II)

1. What did God say when Noah told him he wanted to build the ark out of bricks?

2. What book of the Bible mentions a lousy baseball player?

3. What did Paul do besides preach, teach, and make tents?

4. Who spoke when he was just a baby?

5. Why was Moses buried in the land of Moab?

6. What would have happened to Israel if all the women had left?

7. Which Old Testament prophets were blind?

8. What dishonest musical instrument did David play?

9. What age were the goats when Adam named them in the garden?

10. Who were the twin boys in the Old Testament?

11. In the New Testament?

12. Why was there no alcohol drunk when the Israelites were crossing the Red Sea?

13. Why did Moses cross the Red Sea?

14. Did Noah have a pig in the ark?

15. Who was the fastest runner in the Bible?

16. Where was Solomon's temple?

17. How did Ruth treat Boaz badly?

18. Who rang the first bell?

19. For how long did Cain hate his brother?

20. Who was the most successful doctor in the Bible?

21. Who in the Bible was a very lazy person?

27. Leviticus (22:22).
28. Job (29:15).

✦Not to Be Taken Seriously (II) (Answers)

1. He said, "No, Noah—go for wood [gopherwood]."
2. Psalm 19:12: "Who can understand his errors?"
3. He was a baker, because he went to Philippi (fill a pie).
4. Job—he cursed the day he was born.
5. He was dead.
6. It would have been a stagnation.
7. Hosea, Joel, Amos, Jonah, Nahum, Habbakuk—none of them have i's.
8. The lyre.
9. They were just kids.
10. First and Second Samuel.
11. First and Second Timothy.
12. It was dry land.
13. To avoid Egyptian traffic.
14. Yes—there was Ham.
15. Adam—he was first in the human race.
16. On the side of his head.
17. She pulled his ears and walked on his corn.
18. Cain hit Abel.
19. As long as he was Abel.
20. Job—he had the most patience.
21. The boy that loafs and fishes.

22. Why was a woman in the Old Testament turned into a pillar of salt?

23. As strong as Samson was, what was the one thing he couldn't hold for long?

24. To be baptized by John the Baptist, what did a person have to do?

25. What two things could Samson never have for breakfast?

26. When the ark landed on Ararat, was Noah the first one out?

27. What do you have that Cain and Abel never had?

28. What prophet was a space traveler?

29. How do we know Cain took a nap after he killed Abel?

30. Why didn't Jonah trust the ocean?

31. How long did Samson love Delilah?

32. Who killed a fourth of the people in the world?

33. What was Eve's formal name?

34. When a camel without a hump was born on the ark, what did Noah's wife name him?

35. What was Adam and Eve's phone number?

36. Why did Moses have to be hidden quickly as a baby?

37. What did Samson eat to become strong?

38. If Solomon were alive today, why would he be considered a remarkable man?

39. Who was named after a chicken?

40. Why was the queen of Sheba so impressed by Solomon?

41. What book of the Old Testament has an ugly old woman in its name?

42. Who was the most popular actor in the Bible?

43. What aviator is mentioned in the Bible?

44. When Joseph was in prison in Egypt, what were the names of his cell-mates?

45. When was Adam born?

46. What book mentions a bad pitcher in baseball?

22. She was dissatisfied with her Lot.
23. His breath.
24. Go from bad to immerse.
25. Lunch and dinner.
26. No—he came fourth out of the ark.
27. Grandparents.
28. Elijah—he went up in a fiery chariot.
29. He went to the land of Nod.
30. He knew there was something fishy in it.
31. Until she bald him out.
32. Cain, when he killed Abel.
33. Madam Adam.
34. Humphrey.
35. Adam 8-1-2.
36. Because it was a rush job.
37. Mussels.
38. He would be almost three thousand years old.
39. Hen (Zechariah 6:14).
40. She was amazed that a man with so many wives had the time to write books.
41. (Hag)gai.
42. Samson—he brought the house down.
43. Pilate.
44. Butler and Baker.
45. A little before Eve.
46. Ezekiel 36:12—"Yea, I will cause them to walk."

Other Living Books® Best-sellers

THE ANGEL OF HIS PRESENCE by Grace Livingston Hill. This book captures the romance of John Wentworth Stanley and a beautiful young woman whose influence causes John to re-evaluate his well-laid plans for the future. 07-0047 $3.95.

ANSWERS by Josh McDowell and Don Stewart. In a question-and-answer format, the authors tackle sixty-five of the most-asked questions about the Bible, God, Jesus Christ, miracles, other religions, and creation. 07-0021 $4.95.

THE BEST CHRISTMAS PAGEANT EVER by Barbara Robinson. A delightfully wild and funny story about what happens to a Christmas program when the "Horrible Herdman" brothers and sisters are miscast in the roles of the biblical Christmas story characters. 07-0137 $3.95.

BUILDING YOUR SELF IMAGE by Josh McDowell. Here are practical answers to help you overcome your fears, anxieties, and lack of self-confidence. Learn how God's higher image of who you are can take root in your heart and mind. 07-1395 $4.50.

THE CHILD WITHIN by Mari Hanes. The author shares insights she gained from God's Word during her own pregnancy. She identifies areas of stress, offers concrete data about the birth process, and points to God's sure promises that he will "gently lead those that are with young." 07-0219 $3.95.

COME BEFORE WINTER AND SHARE MY HOPE by Charles R. Swindoll. A collection of brief vignettes offering hope and the assurance that adversity and despair are temporary setbacks we can overcome! 07-0477 $6.95.

DARE TO DISCIPLINE by James Dobson. A straightforward, plainly written discussion about building and maintaining parent/child relationships based upon love, respect, authority, and ultimate loyalty to God. 07-0522 $4.95.

DAVID AND BATHSHEBA by Roberta Kells Dorr. This novel combines solid biblical and historical research with suspenseful storytelling about men and women locked in the eternal struggle for power, governed by appetites they wrestle to control. 07-0618 $4.95.

Other Living Books® Best-sellers

DR. DOBSON ANSWERS YOUR QUESTIONS by James Dobson. In this convenient reference book, renowned author Dr. James Dobson addresses heartfelt concerns on many topics including marital relationships, infant care, child discipline, home management, and others. 07-0580 $4.95.

FOR MEN ONLY edited by J. Allan Petersen. This book deals with topics of concern to every man: the business world, marriage, fathering, spiritual goals, and problems of living as a Christian in a secular world. 07-0892 $4.95.

FOR WOMEN ONLY by Evelyn and J. Allan Petersen. Balanced, entertaining, diversified treatment of all aspects of womanhood. 07-0897 $5.95.

400 WAYS TO SAY I LOVE YOU by Alice Chapin. Perhaps the flame of love has almost died in your marriage. Maybe you have a good marriage that just needs a little "spark." Here is a book especially for the woman who wants to rekindle the flame of romance in her marriage. With creative, practical ideas on how to show the man in her life that she cares. 07-0919 $3.95.

GIVERS, TAKERS, AND OTHER KINDS OF LOVERS by Josh McDowell and Paul Lewis. This book bypasses vague generalities about love and sex and gets right to the basic questions: Whatever happened to sexual freedom? What's true love like? Do men respond differently than women? If you're looking for straight answers about God's plan for love and sexuality, this book was written for you. 07-1031 $3.95.

HINDS' FEET ON HIGH PLACES by Hannah Hurnard. A classic allegory of a journey toward faith that has sold more than a million copies! 07-1429 $4.95.

HOW TO BE HAPPY THOUGH MARRIED by Tim LaHaye. One of America's most successful marriage counselors gives practical, proven advice for marital happiness. 07-1499 $3.95.

JOHN, SON OF THUNDER by Ellen Gunderson Traylor. In this saga of adventure, travel with John—the disciple whom Jesus loved—down desert paths, through the courts of the Holy City, to the foot of the cross, leaving his luxury as a privileged son of Israel for the bitter hardship of his exile on Patmos. 07-1903 $5.95.

Other Living Books® Best-sellers